PACIFIC PROFILES

VOLUME 11
**Allied Fighters: USAAF P-40 Warhawk series
South and Southwest Pacific 1942–1945**

MICHAEL JOHN CLARINGBOULD

Avonmore Books

Pacific Profiles Volume 11

Allied Fighters: USAAF P-40 Warhawk series South and Southwest Pacific 1942–1945

Michael John Claringbould

ISBN: 978-0-6457004-3-5

First published 2023 by Avonmore Books
Avonmore Books
PO Box 217
Kent Town
South Australia 5071
Australia

Phone: (61 8) 8431 9780
avonmorebooks.com.au

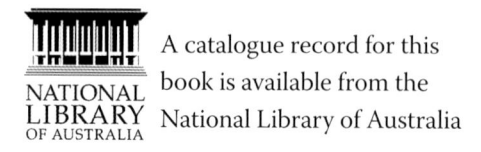

A catalogue record for this book is available from the National Library of Australia

Cover design & layout by Diane Bricknell

© 2023 Avonmore Books.
No part of this book may be reproduced or transmitted in any form or by any means, electronic or mechanical, including photocopying or recording, or by any information storage and retrieval system, without permission in writing from the publisher.

Front Cover: The diversity of markings and P-40 variants is seen in these five Warhawks, top to bottom; an 8th FS P-40N with green chequer-tail, Skeeter a 9th FS Darwin P-40E, a 44th FS shark-mouth, a 35th FS P-40N named Red, and the 9th FS's elusive Texas Longhorn whose identity remained obscure for years. These appear in the publication as Profiles 44, 58, 78, 67 and 61.

Back Cover: A 68th FS P-40F climbs away from Henderson Field in early 1943. A lot of their shark-mouth decorated airframes were later transferred to the 44th FS when the 68th FS converted to Airacobras in June 1943.

Contents

About the Author 5

Introduction 6

Glossary and Abbreviations 11

Chapter 1 – Markings and Technical Notes 13

Chapter 2 – The First P-40s in Australia 23

Chapter 3 – 7th Fighter Squadron "Screamin' Demons" 29

Chapter 4 – 8th Fighter Squadron "The Blacksheep" 45

Chapter 5 – 9th Fighter Squadron "Flying Knights" 57

Chapter 6 – 35th Fighter Squadron "Black Panthers" 69

Chapter 7 – 44th Fighter Squadron "Vampires" 75

Chapter 8 – 68th Fighter Squadron 87

Chapter 9 – 110th Tactical Reconnaissance Squadron "Musketeers" 93

Chapter 10 – 312th Bombardment Group 97

Chapter 11 – Unique Warhawks 101

Sources & Acknowledgments 105

Index of Names 106

The author (centre) in Port Moresby on 18 July 2004 with (left) historian John Douglas and Justin Taylan (right), owner of website www.pacificwrecks.com.

About the Author

Michael Claringbould – Author & Illustrator

Michael spent his formative years in Papua New Guinea in the 1960s, during which he became fascinated by the many WWII aircraft wrecks which lay around the country and also throughout the Solomon Islands. Michael subsequently served widely overseas as an Australian diplomat throughout Southeast Asia and the Pacific, including in Fiji (1995-1998) and Papua New Guinea (2003-2005). Michael's history of the Tainan Naval Air Group in New Guinea, *Eagles of the Southern Sky*, received worldwide acclaim as the first English-language history of a Japanese fighter unit, and was subsequently translated into Japanese. An executive member of Pacific Air War History Associates, Michael holds a pilot license and PG4 paraglider rating. He continues to develop his skills as a digital aviation artist.

Other Books by the Author

Black Sunday – Second Edition - When the US Fifth Air Force Lost to the Weather (2022)

Eagles of the Southern Sky – history of the Tainan Naval Air Group (2012, with Luca Ruffato)

Nemoto's Travels –The illustrated saga of an IJN floatplane pilot (2021)

Operation I-Go – Yamamoto's Last Offensive – New Guinea & Solomons April 1943 (2020)

Pacific Adversaries Series

Vol One – Japanese Army Air Force vs Allies New Guinea 1942-1944 (2019)

Vol Two – Imperial Japanese Navy vs Allies New Guinea & Solomons 1942-1944 (2020)

Vol Three – Imperial Japanese Navy vs Allies New Guinea & the Solomons 1942-1944 (2020)

Vol Four – Imperial Japanese Navy vs Allies – The Solomons 1943-1944 (2021)

Pacific Profiles Series

Vol One Japanese Army Fighters New Guinea & the Solomons 1942-1944 (2020)

Vol Two Japanese Army Bomber & Other Units, New Guinea & Solomons 1942-44 (2020)

Vol Three Allied Medium Bombers, A-20 Series, South West Pacific 1942-44 (2020)

Vol Four Allied Fighters: Vought F4U Corsair Series Solomons Theatre 1943-1944 (2021)

Vol Five Zero Fighters (land-based) New Guinea & Solomons 1942-1944 (2021)

Vol Six Allied Fighters: Bell Airacobra South & Southwest Pacific 1942-1944 (2022)

Vol Seven Allied Transports: Douglas C-47 South & Southwest Pacific 1942-1945 (2022)

Vol Eight – Japanese Floatplanes in the Pacific 1942-45 (2022)

Vol Nine – P-38 Series, SWPA and SOPAC theatres 1942-44 (2022)

Vol 10 – P-47D Series, SWPA, 1943-45 (2023)

South Pacific Air War Series (with Peter Ingman)

Volume 1: The Fall of Rabaul December 1941–March 1942 (2017)

Volume 2: The Struggle for Moresby March–April 1942 (2018)

Volume 3: Coral Sea & Aftermath May–June 1942 (2019)

Volume 4: Buna & Milne Bay June-September 1942 (2020)

Volume 5: Crisis in Papua September – December 1942 (2022)

Solomons Air War Series (with Peter Ingman)

Volume 1: Guadalcanal – August-September 1942 (2023)

Osprey Publications

P-39 / P-400 Airacobra versus A6M2/3 Zero-sen New Guinea 1942 (2018)

F4U Corsair versus A6M2/3/4 Zero-sen, Solomons and Rabaul 1943-44 (2022)

P-47D Thunderbolt versus Ki-43 Hayabusa New Guinea 1943/44 (2020)

A6M2/3 Zero-sen – New Guinea 1942 – Dogfight Series (2023)

Operation Ro – November 1943 - Campaign Series (2023)

Introduction

Welcome to the treacherous complexity of the USAAF P-40 series which served in Australia, New Guinea and the South Pacific.[1] Given that the type's length of service spans the entire duration of the Pacific War, the markings varied through numerous changes of those times. This volume seeks to clarify these markings through the inclusion of a suite of new profiles which showcases the diversity which ensued.

It must be underlined that, whilst both the RAAF and RNZAF operated P-40s in substantial numbers, neither of these services are represented in this volume which focuses exclusively on USAAC/USAAF units. Similar to Japanese practice, individual fighters were flown by different pilots as the needs of the day dictated. In practical terms airframes were assigned to crew chiefs rather than pilots. In the SWPA, USAAF P-40s mostly engaged the Japanese Army Air Force (JAAF), whilst in the SOPAC theatre they fought almost exclusively Japanese Navy units, the rare exception being JAAF involvement in the January 1943 Operation *Ke* campaign over Guadalcanal. Some familiar fighters of the "aces" are included; however, these pilots did not always fly their particular "assigned" fighter all the time. Relevant to the SWPA and SOPAC theatres, actual losses confirmed in Japanese operations logs indicate on average that US claims can be divided by three to four, each circumstance of course being individual. Note that Japanese combat claims were even more ambitious.

When the Australian government foresaw the collapse of the Netherlands East Indies (NEI), it first sought US government agreement to purchase "Tomahawks" with no P-40 model quoted. Thereafter a request was made for "Kittyhawks" on 31 January 1942. Both types had proven combat credentials earned from both RAF and RAAF service in the Middle East, noting that No. 3 Squadron, RAAF, was the first Australian squadron to fly the Kittyhawk Mk 1 from December 1941. The British P-40E-1 export version performed badly above 14,000 feet and was accordingly viewed poorly by the USAAC. The last P-40E-1 was delivered in June 1942. No P-40B Tomahawk found its way to Australia or the Pacific, although for some reason one set of stray wings did.

The Warhawk was the first modern fighter to enter service in the early NEI and Philippine theatres, followed by the Australian theatre before the type became ubiquitous in the Pacific. Following the invasion of the Philippines, subsequent batches of P-40Es were delivered to Java in small numbers via Australia, several of which later re-appear in USAAF and RAAF Pacific squadrons. Due to the heavy USAAC losses incurred in the Philippines and Java, in April 1942 P-40E airframes which had originally been earmarked for RAAF usage were "repossessed" by the USAAF and reassigned to the 49th PG at Darwin. These airframes constituted payback for 81 P-40E/E-1s issued earlier from the US Foreign Aid "Project X" inventory.

By September 1942 combat losses saw the 49th FG Warhawk inventory reduced to 64, a reduced number from the group's official allocation of 80. Their replacements led to further markings

---

[1] For the purposes of this volume the South West Pacific Area (SWPA) means Australia and New Guinea, while SOPAC refers to the adjoining South Pacific theatre. The USAAF Fifth Air Force served in the SWPA while the Thirteenth Air Force served in SOPAC.

INTRODUCTION

complexity. Between December 1941 and October 1942, a substantive total of 571 P-40E and E-1 British lend-lease variants was delivered to Australia. By May 1943 the Fifth Air Force had only 54 of this original allocation of early model Warhawks remaining on strength, and by 1944 this total had been reduced to a handful serving in support and ancillary roles, including as two-seat trainers.

The competing demands of RAAF squadrons and high operational accident rates in all units led to considerable inventory exchanges between Warhawk units. Such exchanges continued at feverish pace throughout 1942, resulting in widespread ramifications for markings. These in turn have resulted in considerable markings confusion. The Fifth Air Force created a maintenance headquarters, the Fighter Replacement Pool, specifically to coordinate these transfers. In July 1942 the pool relocated to Garbutt near Townsville from Williamtown in New South Wales. During the move all USAAF Brewster Buffalos on charge were given to the RAAF, however its CW-22 Falcons and refitted P-40E/E-1s moved north with the unit. A subsidiary joint RAAF/USAAF replacement pool was subsequently established at Charleville, north Queensland, to assist with this process.

Many of the early P-40E series airframes left in Australia following the 49th FG's move to New Guinea at the end of 1942 were reallocated to the RAAF or subsidiary USAAF units via these facilities. When the Garbutt operation expanded in late 1942 to include yet more maintenance units, it was renamed the Fighter Command Replacement Center (FCRC). The move to New Guinea of the 49th FG's three squadrons further complicated markings matters. The 7th FS was the exclusive beneficiary from an October 1942 shipment of 35 new P-40K-5s, although some were retained at Townsville's FCRC alongside a suite of refitted P-40E/E-1s. In December 1942 when the 9th FS converted to the Lockheed Lightning, its entire Warhawk inventory was transferred to Townsville. This transition incurred rancor when a contingent of former ex-Java 17th PS pilots was assigned into the 9th FS and given the first P-38s as soon as they became available. This left many of the squadron's Darwin-veteran pilots languishing in Townsville throughout October 1942 lamenting the loss of their P-40s. Finally, informed that the P-38's entry to combat had been delayed, the 9th FS then took most of its Warhawks to New Guinea too. In the event, the final 9th FS Warhawk combat took place on 31 December 1942.

Meanwhile up in New Guinea, new P-40 airframes were transferred to the 8th FS via the FCRC's maintenance group, the 45th Service Group, resulting in mixed 7th and 8th FS inventories. Then, by mid-1943 in New Guinea, the 7th FS was reassigned former 8th FS refits to replace its dwindling supply of P-40K-5s. The last P-40E to see combat in New Guinea was operated by the 7th FS, being P-40E-1 ET494 flown by Second Lieutenant Logan Jarmen. He claimed a bomber on 14 July 1943 when flying this fighter, the last "E" model to make a combat claim.

We now turn to the SOPAC theatre where the short-fuselage P-40F-1 with its distinctive square-shaped cowl without top air scoop first appeared in the New Hebrides in November 1942. These were followed by the extended fuselage variant P-40F-15 in June 1943. The "F" model series with its unique Rolls-Royce engine installation presented several engineering challenges, however no "F" models made it to the SWPA.

The P-40M first arrived in the SOPAC theatre in August 1943 with the 44th FS. Several 70th FS pilots were seconded to the 44th FS to gain combat experience in the type at this juncture. Only a handful of "M" models wound up in USAAF service in the SWPA, one being illustrated in Profile 110. The "M" model was, however, ubiquitous in both the RAAF and RNZAF inventories.

The first "N" models appeared in New Guinea in September 1943, and ushered in a new era of markings, but oddly these were P-40N-5s, not P-40N-1s, which served exclusively in the SOPAC theatre, making their debut in Guadalcanal in December 1943. In New Guinea the ubiquitous N-5 immediately swelled the ranks of the 7th, 8th and 35th FS. The first P-40N-15s and P-40N-20s appeared in June 1944 which included twenty former RAAF airframes, just when USAAF Warhawk units were about to vacate New Guinea. The first P-40N-30 appeared at Morotai in the NEI a few months later. Late-model P-40Ns and P-40Ms were still in Pacific service by war's end, mainly serving in ground support roles. Even the occasional old-timer P-40E remained active at the end of the war serving as a hack, photo-ship or commandeered by maintenance units to ferry parts and documents.

Finally, a word of caution. The degree to which airframes were traded and transferred between units was extreme. It was commonplace for a squadron to have three to five airframes every month taken offline while they were repaired, let alone those lost in combat or side-lined due to a lack of parts. If the repairs required were sufficiently substantial the fighter would be given to a service squadron, before often re-entering service with a different combat unit. As such, it was commonplace for many P-40s to have undergone two to three markings schemes, even within the same squadron. Thus, it can be difficult to be definitive about particular airframe markings unless a particular timeframe is nominated. In most cases photographic evidence covering broader timeframes is deficient.

Michael John Claringbould
Canberra, Australia
May 2023

FIFTH AIR FORCE
P-40 Main Bases
1942/44

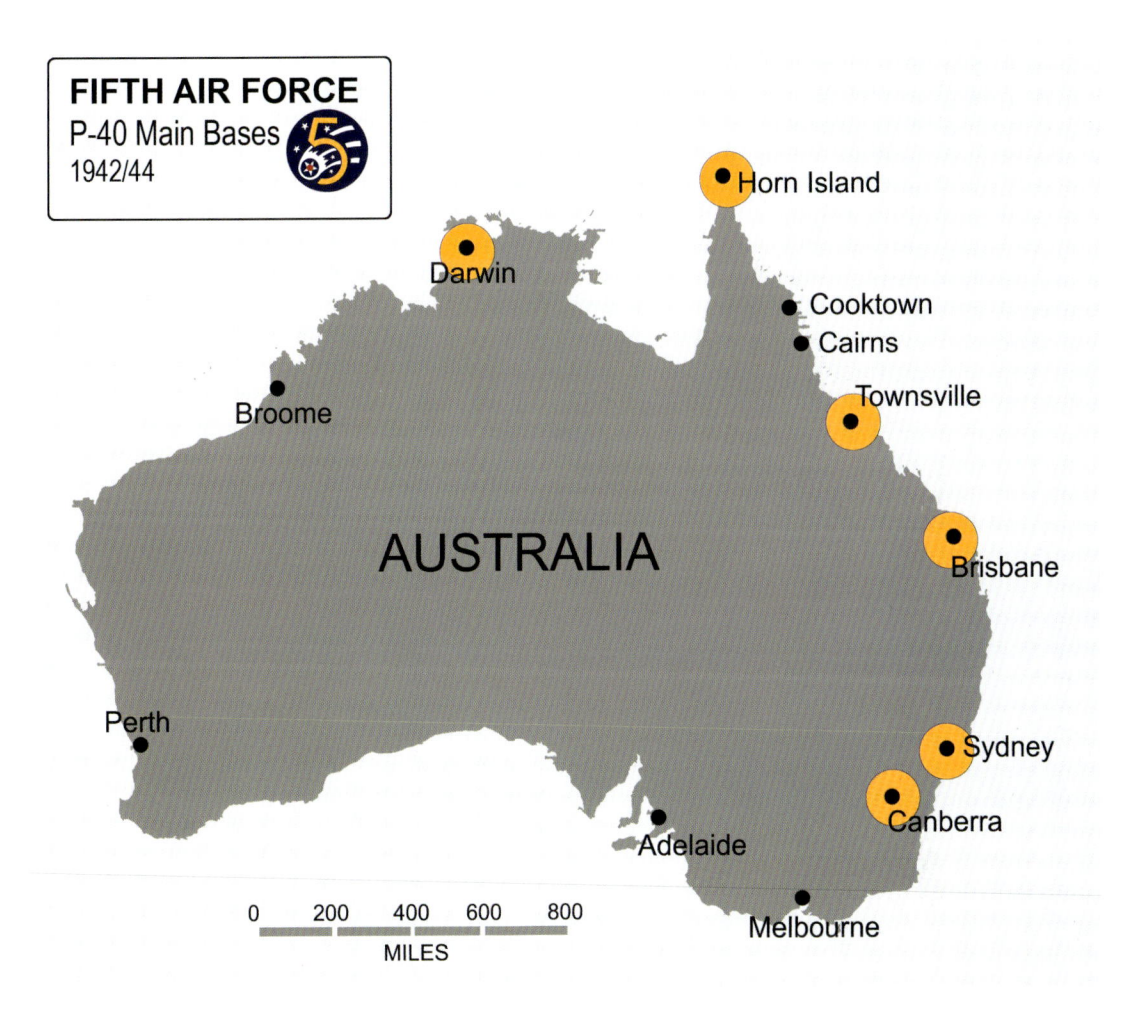

The first P-40s to arrive in Australia were assembled at RAAF Amberley near Brisbane in January 1942 and were followed by hundreds of others. A number were flown to Java via Darwin in January and February 1942 before that route was cut off by the Japanese advance. From March 1942 P-40Es of the 49th PG/FG saw combat over Horn Island and Darwin. Later that year the 49th FG advanced to New Guinea and the air defence of the Australian continent became a wholly RAAF responsibility. However, Australia remained an important base for USAAF P-40 maintenance operations, especially Townsville which became home to a large training pool.

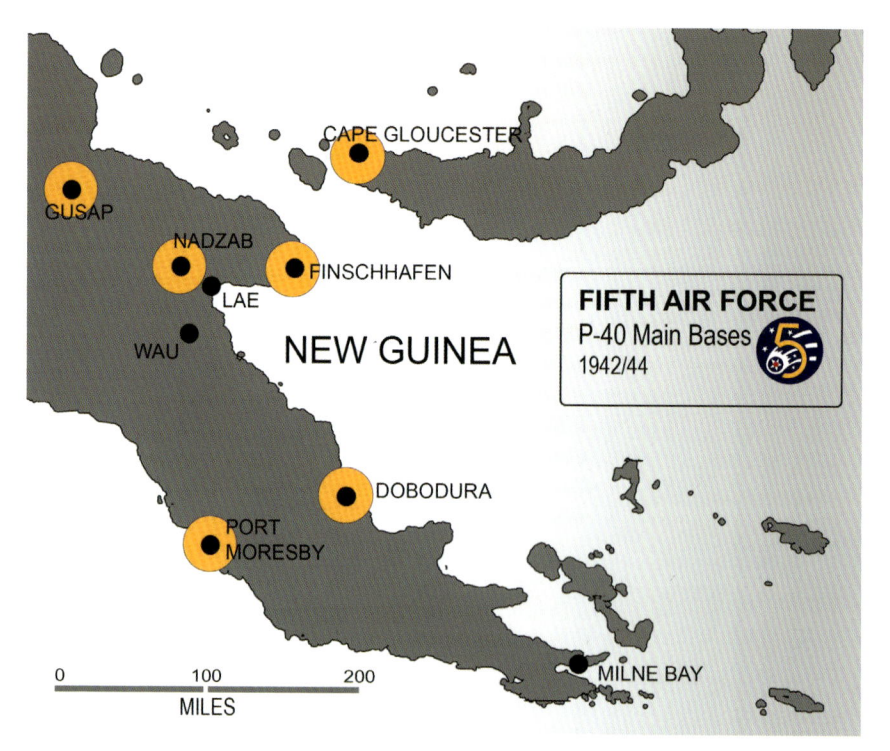

A map showing key airbases used by Fifth Air Force P-40s in the New Guinea area of the South West Pacific Area command during 1942-1944. Note that some of these locations had several airfields. For example, Port Moresby hosted six sizeable airfields: Three-Mile (Kila), Five-Mile (Wards), Seven-Mile (Jacksons), 12-Mile (Berry), 14-Mile (Schwimmer) and 17-Mile (Durand).

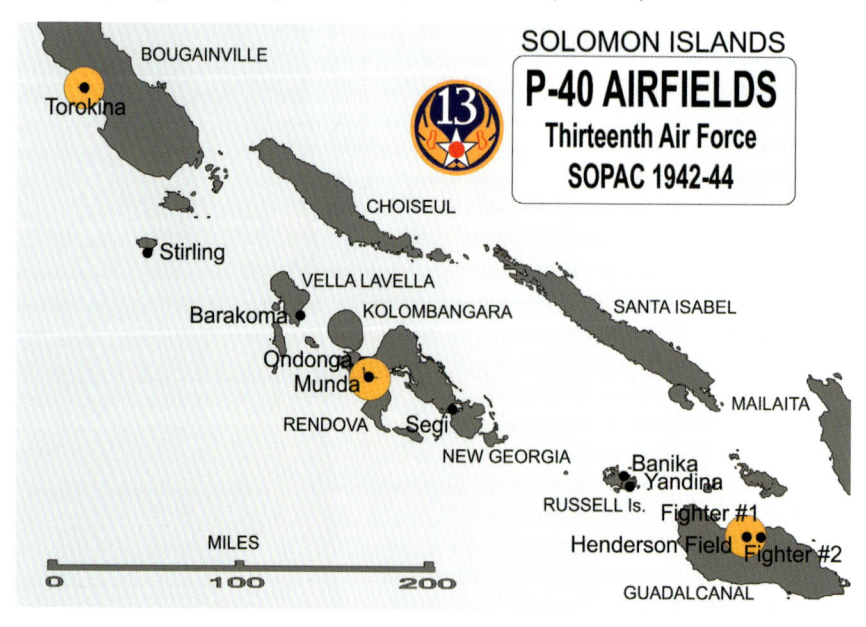

A map showing key airbases used by Thirteenth Air Force P-40s in the Solomons area of the South Pacific Area command during 1942-1944.

Glossary and Abbreviations

BG	Bombardment Group
BS	Bombardment Squadron
FCRC	Fighter Command Replacement Center
FEAF	Far East Air Force
FG	Fighter Group
FPO1c	Flying Petty Officer First Class
FS	Fighter Squadron
Hinomaru	The red disc on the Japanese flag representing the sun and also used as a roundel on Japanese aircraft.
JAAF	Japanese Army Air Force
Kokutai	A Japanese naval air group
Ku	Abbreviation of *Kokutai*
NEI	Netherlands East Indies
NFS	Night Fighter Squadron
PG	Pursuit Group
PS	Pursuit Squadron
RAAF	Royal Australian Air Force
RNZAF	Royal New Zealand Air Force
Sentai	Abbreviation of *hiko sentai* defining a JAAF flying regiment.
SOPAC	South Pacific Area
SWPA	South West Pacific Area
TRS	Tactical Reconnaissance Squadron
US	United States
USN	United States Navy
USAAC	United States Army Air Corps
USAAF	United States Army Air Force

The first P-40E assembled at RAAF Amberley, near Brisbane, in January 1942 from a batch originally intended for delivery to the Philippines.

An RAAF P40E-1 as delivered with 1941 yellow-outline RAF roundels which were subsequently painted over in RAAF or later USAAF service. These RAF-contract models were delivered with white spinners.

CHAPTER 1
Markings and Technical Notes

Technical

Several technical peculiarities need to be highlighted to explain various associated markings variations. The P-40E and P-40E-1 had interchangeable top and lower cowlings. Many other parts were exchangeable, including circular and "fishtail" exhausts, and this convenience produces ongoing identification problems (as a rule the Allison engine V-1710-73 series onwards had fishtail exhausts). It is thus no surprise that superlative and thus coveted artwork on cowls was commandeered during unit transfers. Two examples are the cowls of *Skeeter* and *Texas Longhorn* (Profiles 58 and 61), one of which even appears on a later RAAF Kittyhawk!

The first 800 P40E-1s, British serials ET100 to ET999, had one upper and one lower formation light mounted flush into the fuselage forward of the cockpit. Early P-40Es had none, neither did the first 400 P-40N-1s. Many E and E-1 variants which survived early combat were modified/refitted by the 43rd Service Squadron in Australia, including an extension of the head plate from the pilot's shoulders to the upper forearm. Both models were configured to carry one centreline 500-pound demolition bomb or drop-tank, however later provision was made on several P-40E-1s by modifying hardpoints to carry differing bomb loads, including six 21-pound wing-mounted bombs.

The RAAF experimented with field modifications on later P-40Ns to improve the bomb loads, and this knowledge was shared with USAAF service units. This involved replacing the outer machine gun panels with a thickened hard-point plate to replace the outer gun mount and the associated 0.50-inch calibre machine gun. The modification enabled the carriage of 300-pound bombs and was designed so that the armament could be reconfigured in the field back to a six-gun arrangement if desired. The P40N-1 was delivered with four 0.50-inch calibre machine guns installed, and two more cased in the shipping box, enabling it to be easily converted to a six-gun platform. Pilots sometimes preferred the four-gun configuration if also toting bombs. Finally, many N-5s had wing hard points installed so they could carry an extra drop tank for long-range missions or ferrying. In summary, it can be challenging to definitely ascertain a P-40 model from photographs due to *inter alia* repaints, field modifications, refits and part swaps, especially in respect to cowls and rudders.

P-40E, F, M and the later N models left the factory in Olive Drab with Neutral Grey underneath. Later batches had a green overspray applied to the leading and trailing edges of the tailplane and wings, sprayed using medium pressure against a rubber template. Both the P40E-1 and P-40K-1 were generally completed in the Dupont Paint Corporation scheme, an equivalent of the RAF Sand and Dark Green camouflage scheme with a Sky Blue undersurface. However, to further complicate matters, a limited number of P-40K-1s and P-40E-1s left the factory in Olive Drab. Dupont's colours varied slightly to the equivalent RAF ones, however, note that the two-tone camouflage scheme is often indiscernible in black and white photos, particularly where the sun is behind the subject. Darwin pilots affectionately referred to this scheme as "sand and spinach".

As a result of transition though RAAF overhaul units, service depots and the FCRC, many P-40s in Australia and New Guinea were repainted in a variety of both RAAF and workshop schemes. These included customised Olive Drab, two-tone camouflage or overall foliage green applications. This explains why several P-40E-1s and P-40K-1s appear in Olive Drab schemes, their Australian equivalent, or vice-versa. In particular several P40E-1s which transited the USAAF 43rd Service Squadron for refit were sprayed in Olive Drab or foliage green, explaining why foliage green P-40s appear in the 8th FS New Guinea inventory. These resprays were unique as formal directives were either non-existent, suitably flexible or ignored during application.

Early P-40Es often arrived with their box number stenciled on the tailplane in white or black. These box numbers can be confused with squadron numbers or partial serial numbers, however there is no relation between the three. Examples of box numbers are illustrated in Figure 3 (see page 20, examples 14 and 15) and Profiles 4 and 5.

Box numbers were applied only to those leaving the factory in crates; however, the practice was soon discontinued, but variances became widespread. All pre-January 1942 Russia-destined P-40E/P-40E-1s had only data plates, with no serial numbers prior to leaving the factory. A limited number found their way to Australia in boxes. In such cases the Curtiss-Wright customer sequence number was the only means of identifying each airframe. The concept, naive or not, was that its USAAF provenance could not be proven if captured.

Theater Tailplane Markings

As early as July 1943 both the Fifth and Thirteenth Air Forces painted fighter tailplanes all-white, including wing leading edges. However, as illustrated, both the 44th and 68th FS at first applied white stripe markings to wings and tailplanes before the all-white scheme became common practice. Shortages of white paint saw water-based or acrylic applications, resulting in a heavily weathered appearance, especially where polymer emulsions failed to bond with polyurethane factory bases. The marking's purpose was so that Allied fighters, ships and gunnery units could more easily identify these fighters as "friendlies". Although the Fifth Air Force official directive to apply the markings was promulgated in September 1943 via Washington, the directive is a showcase *de facto* example of a field initiative being formalised by headquarters after the fact.

Insignia

All P-40Es left the factory with the early, red-centered roundel US insignia and the large stenciled "U.S. ARMY" applied under the wing, facing forward and in dark blue (not black as often misrepresented). Some batches of P40E-1s had British roundel stencils included in the delivery crate pending application, so were unpacked without any national insignia, and were affixed with clear dope. A limited number of early P40E-1s arrived with 1941 yellow-outline RAF roundels. These were transferred to the RAAF among the 125 redirected to lend-lease allocations as illustrated in Profile 3. By the time these found their way into USAAF service the yellow surround was long gone. Nonetheless when such airframes reappear in US units their faded legacy yellow can sometimes be seen.

The first Warhawks assigned to the 49th PG at Darwin made the first stage of their journey without any insignia. It was later painted on via stencils at the Fighter Replacement Pool at Charleville.

Orders issued to the 49th Pursuit Group on 27 March 1942 instructed the eradication of the red centre on all US insignia, lest it be mistaken for a Japanese *hinomaru* in the flash of battle. Even before this edict, several 3rd PS (Provisional) pilots had seen fit to minimise the red circle, or even eradicate it, an example seen in Profile 2. However, there was also a time lag of up to several weeks before these measures were fully implemented. The P40N-1 and early batches of the N-5 had USAAF roundels without bars applied at the factory. White bars were later added in the field by Fifth and Thirteenth Air Force service units.

Box number 210 seen on a P-40 at Darwin in early 1942. Note the pattern on the airframe is produced by shadowing from the camouflage netting.

PACIFIC PROFILES

FIGURE 1 - Model Variations

P-40E-1

P-40K

P-40E

P-40F-1

P-40F-15

P-40M & N-1

P-40N-5

P-40N-15

ET443

Figure 1 – Model Variations: When they left the factory all P-40 variants (illustrated to scale) incorporated unique design and markings features. Neither were these always consistent, dependent on the precise model number, later dash series and contract number. This comparative chart circles only the more significant markings and design features common to factory specification models and is by no means comprehensive.

P-40E-1: This British export model had a Dupont Sky coloured undersurface and left the production line with a British serial, but only if consigned as a "DA3" contract. All shipped to Australia lay in the ET series, however most of those sent to Tonga with the 68th FS were in the EV series. This latter series was the first batch of P-40E-1s which was on-shipped to New Caledonia from Australia in May 1942, and left the factory with "US ARMY" stencilled in dark blue letters on the undersurface.

P-40K-1: The K-1 model had a more powerful engine installed, along with "fish-tail" exhausts, and as such the root of the fin was increased to provide extra directional stability. Although most left the factory in two-tone brown and Medium Green, those contracted directly for the USAAF were finished in Olive Drab and Medium Green. A curious modification exception is that P-40E-1s from British serial EV151 onwards were also factory fitted with the extended fin and fillet. The first P-40K-1 arrived in the SWPA in October 1942.

P-40E: The E model was by far the most ubiquitous in the SWPA throughout 1942. It left the factory with "US ARMY" stencilled in dark blue letters on the undersurface.

P-40F-1: All F models had a Rolls-Royce Merlin installed and lacked the forward dorsal air intake of the E model, and thus had a different-shaped cowl. The F model only served in the SOPAC theatre. Other than firewall-forward modifications, the F-1 was essentially an E airframe backwards from the firewall.

P-40F-15: Later F models had an extended fuselage with forward-placed tailplane to enhance pitch control. Still equipped with the Rolls-Royce Merlin, it also lacked the upper air intake but shared the same cowl as the F-1. The leading edges of its fin and wings were camouflaged with dark foliage green. The extended F model was a precursor to all the later P-40 series with the extended fuselage.

P-40M & N-1: The M model reverted to the Allison engine and thus incorporated the top air scoop. Along with the P-40N-1, it was the last model with the "scallop" cockpit and, aside from service with the RAAF and RNZAF, it served primarily in the SOPAC theatre. The P40N-1 was the lightest and fastest of the N series. A handful of P-40Ms was delivered to the Fifth Air Force as Thirteenth Air Force reassignments. Note top and bottom aerial installations.

P-40N-5: Designed from lessons learnt during aerial combat in both Australia and the Pacific, the N-5 series incorporated a redesigned cockpit to enhance rear visibility. Both the N-1 and early N-5 appeared without a bar to the national insignia. These were field-applied shortly after delivery to the theatre.

P-40N-15: The P40N-15 series onwards left the factory with the star and bar and included a suite of airframe modifications including modified hard points. These made the airframe heavier and more suitable for ground attack, but less maneuverable than the early N models.

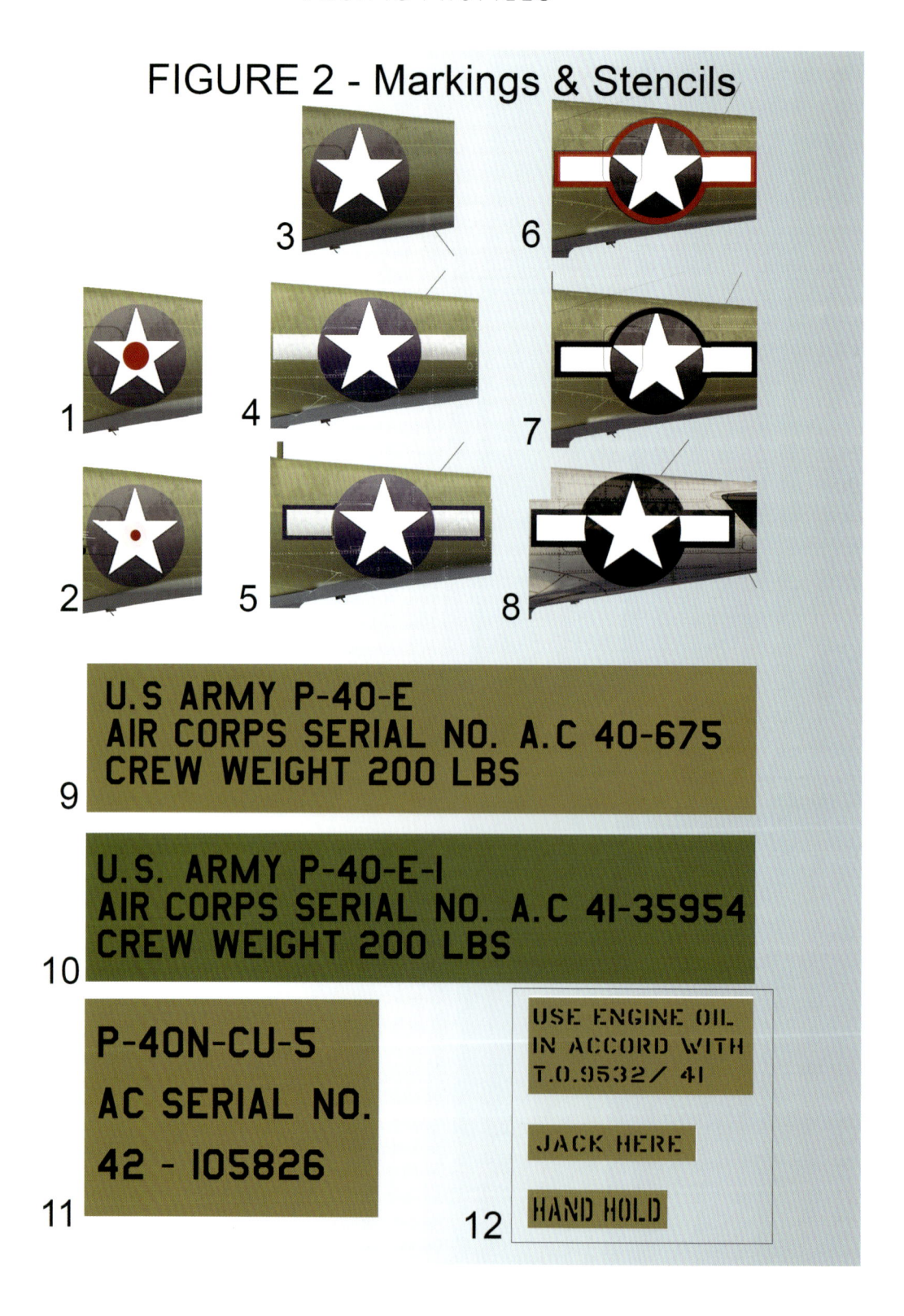

FIGURE 2 - Markings & Stencils

9
U.S ARMY P-40-E
AIR CORPS SERIAL NO. A.C 40-675
CREW WEIGHT 200 LBS

10
U.S. ARMY P-40-E-I
AIR CORPS SERIAL NO. A.C 41-35954
CREW WEIGHT 200 LBS

11
P-40N-CU-5
AC SERIAL NO.
42 - 105826

12
USE ENGINE OIL
IN ACCORD WITH
T.O.9532/41

JACK HERE

HAND HOLD

Figure 2 – Markings and Stencils

Example 1: The standard US insignia which appeared on all P-40E airframes leaving US factories prior to May 1942.

Example 2: This field-modified Example 1 served to minimise (or eradicate) the red centre in the insignia. It was first applied to several airframes in Australia as early as February 1942.

Example 3: The standard US insignia, without red centre, leaving US factories from May 1942 through to May 1943.

Examples 4 and 5: The single circular insignia with white bars added in the field to all aircraft types by both the Fifth and Thirteenth Air Forces. Later in the war these white bars had blue, black or grey piping added (see Example 8).

Example 6: Back in the mainland US, army tests had concluded shapes were easier to discern than colours, so bars with red piping were added to accentuate the insignia. The Army/Navy (AN) Markings Specification AN-1-9A promulgated on 28 June 1943 ordered red-bordered insignia applied to all USAAF aircraft in July 1943.

Example 7: Due to the colour association with the *hinomaru*, the Fifth Air Force informed Washington in August 1943 that it was removing all red borders on security grounds. Both the Fifth and Thirteenth Air Forces had in fact already commenced doing this with appropriate dark-coloured paint stocks at hand.

Example 8: On 14 August 1943 a dark blue outline insignia with bars was ordered per the AN-I-9A specification. Then, Technical Order 07-1-1 issued on 24 September 1943 ordered applying blue piping to extant field markings, however these had already been implemented by Warhawk units in the field. Production runs commencing with late batches of the P-40N-5 onwards left the factory with this insignia.

USAAF Manufacturer's Stencil: This stencil appeared only on the forward port fuselage side underneath the cockpit and is the Curtiss-Wright Corporation manufacturing stencil. All Warhawks were manufactured at the company's plant in Buffalo, New York. Even though the USAAF issued guidelines on stencil formats and sizes, these could differ slightly in practice according to production runs.

Example 9 and 10: The P-40E-1 carried both a USAAF stencil in addition to a British serial on the rear fuselage.

Example 11: The simplified stencil for later N series production runs. "CU" represents "Curtiss".

Example 12: These self-explanatory stencils appeared on different parts of the airframe. Ground crews in the field often reapplied stencils in white so they were easier to read, or made new ones following field modifications, particularly on field-modified shackle and tank release systems.

FIGURE 3 - USAAF Tailplane Box & Serial Numbers

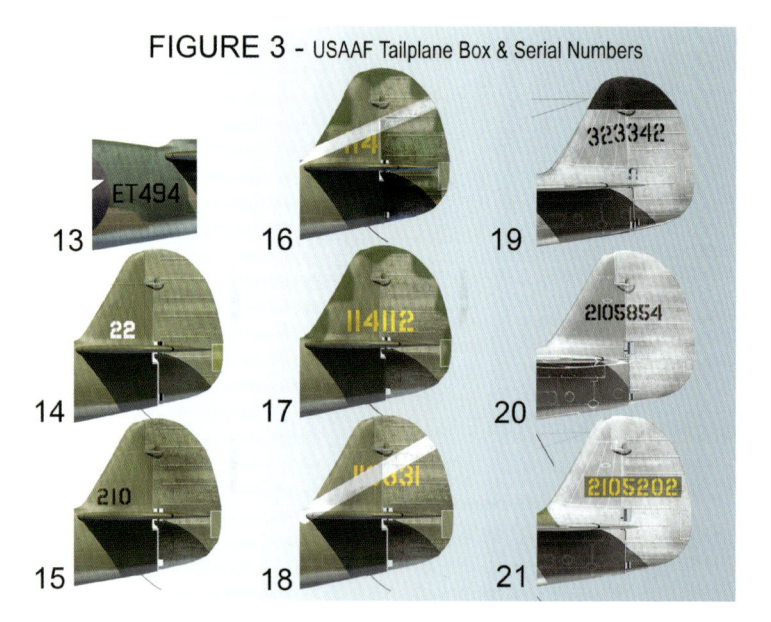

Figure 3 - USAAF Box and Tailplane Serial Numbers Numerous variations apply to the factory stencil style applied to the fin, depending on the batch run and model number. These were often replaced or modified in the field when reapplied over white tails or following repairs. Early batches of P-40Es left the factory with only box numbers applied, and British E-1s had a British serial on the rear fuselage instead, although they retained a manufacturer's stencil as per Example 10. Many camouflaged K models left the factory with serial number stencils on the fin too.

Example 13: A British serial with its unique font type.

Example 14 and 15: Box number examples, applied in both white and black.

Example 16: Sometimes when a rudder was replaced, the rest of the serial was not applied, such as appears on this P-40F-1.

Example 17: The P-40F and P-40K factory runs had larger stencils applied lower on the fin than later models.

Example 18: The white oblique stripe applied across the serial number of Thirteenth Air Force P-40s. In late June 1943 these were replaced by all-white tailplanes.

Example 19: A field stencil as applied by service squadrons from Port Moresby to Nadzab. This particular example is skewed.

Example 20: A field-applied stencil applied over an all-white tail, replicating the Curtiss-Wright factory style.

Example 21: This P-40N-5 used a mask to retain the original serial number when the white tail was painted. This was a practice commonly observed by the 35th FS, however less so by other Fifth Air Force units on later model P-40s.

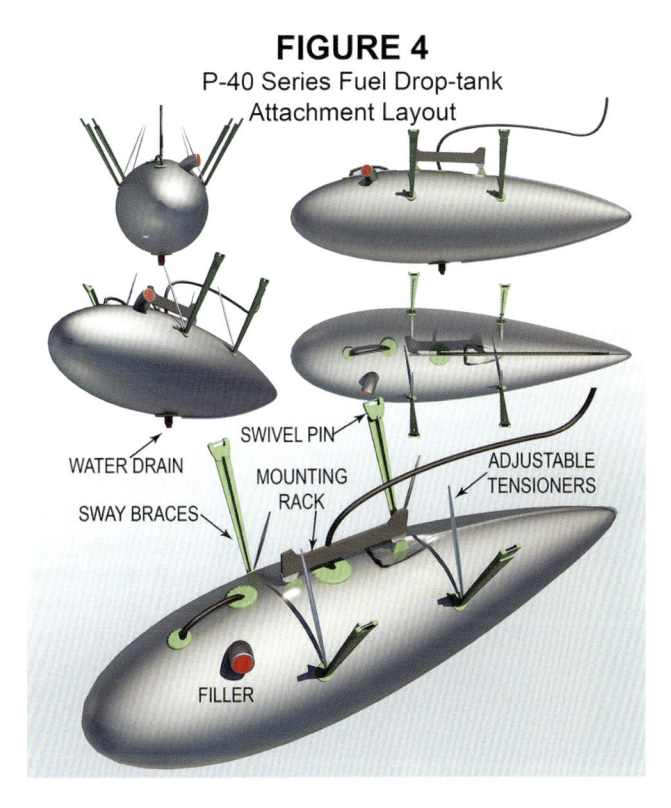

FIGURE 4
P-40 Series Fuel Drop-tank Attachment Layout

WATER DRAIN
SWAY BRACES
SWIVEL PIN
MOUNTING RACK
ADJUSTABLE TENSIONERS
FILLER

Figure 4 - Drop Tank and Attachment The P-40 series could tote either a 52, 75 or 150 US gallon tank, retained by a central ventral hardpoint, and stabilised by four sway braces (see Figure 4). This same hardpoint could lug either a 100- or 300-pound bomb, and later modifications enabled the carriage of heavier bombs. The first 225 P-40Es lacked self-sealing tanks, thereafter all subsequent P40E-1s were equipped with metal fuel tanks with self-sealing liners. The P-40N series was equipped with non-metal self-sealing tanks which catered for aromatic fuel. P40E/E-1 tanks were lined with a Fuller compound which broke down when exposed to high octane fuel, causing these liners to be replaced. The N series was delivered with the rear wing tanks and fuselage tank, reducing their capacity from the E model series from 156 US gallons to 120 US gallons. Thus, the P-40N usually carried the larger 75 US gallon drop tank. However, this often proved unpractical for combat, and instead the 52 US gallon tank was used to ensure a 200-mile operational range.

By August 1943 a field-designed 200 US gallon tank was being manufactured in Brisbane by the Ford Motor Company which was known colloquially as the "Brisbane Tank". Although originally manufactured for the Republic P-47D, its release and mounting mechanisms were soon fabricated, and booster pumps designed for P-40 tanks provided fuel transfer. Later in the war units started replacing the 200-gallon "Brisbane tank" with a field-designed 160-gallon wing-mounted fuel drop-tank around late January 1944. Many P-40Ns were field-modified to carry two or even three drop tanks, increasing the extra fuel capacity to 320 gallons. The shape and size of the fuel tanks on the P-40 series thus varied considerably depending on the timeframe and theatre, modification sequence and type.

Early 13th PS (Provisional) P-40Es about to depart Richmond in New South Sales on their cross-country flight to Freemantle in Western Australia in mid-February 1942. Box numbers 23, 35 and (white) 7 are among the P-40Es, with an RAAF Beaufort visible in the background. After being loaded onto the old carrier USS Langley at Freemantle, these Warhawks were lost when that ship was sunk south of Java on 27 February.

Second Lieutenant John Glover's Dumbo (the subject of Profile 5) following its crash at Darwin on 19 February 1942.

CHAPTER 2
The First P-40s in Australia

The fast-encroaching Japanese advances forced a rethink of where to redeploy impending P-40E deliveries, resulting in a decision to divert them to Australia. In late November 1941 a reinforcement convoy set sail for the Philippines from San Francisco. Named after its escort cruiser the USS *Pensacola*, the "Pensacola Convoy" carried cargo including eighteen crated P-40Es and 52 A-24 dive-bombers. In a complex command structure, the umbrella unit of the shipment was the 35th PG whose headquarters was placed temporarily under the 24th PG. The Warhawks were destined for the 3rd, 17th, 20th and 21st Pursuit Squadrons in the Philippines.

At this juncture it is important to understand the timeline of "Project X", the urgent reinforcement of the Philippines, appropriately codenamed SUMAC for "Send Urgently MacArthur". At a November 1941 conference it had been decided that should the Japanese blockade maritime supply routes to the Philippines, then aircraft could be assembled in Townsville. However due to the lack of RAAF infrastructure there, as mentioned above the Pensacola Convoy was rerouted to Brisbane, where the P-40Es and A-24s could be assembled and test flown from nearby RAAF Amberley.

The convoy docked at Brisbane's wharves on 22 December 1941 where the ships unloaded the aircraft. All were transported to RAAF Amberley some forty miles distant where they were reassembled by the RAAF's No. 3 Service Flying Training School, alongside the USAAC 8th Materiel Squadron. P-40E serial 41-5332 was the first Warhawk to be test flown on 2 January 1942. Subsequent aircraft were erected within a fortnight, however there were various challenges including sourcing Prestone coolant.

Then, in the first week of January 1942 the planned single-engine ferry route to the Philippines was cut off due to Japanese moves in the northern NEI. Meanwhile an American-British-Dutch-Australia command had been created to coordinate the defence of the NEI. All surviving 19th BG Flying Fortresses in the Philippines were ferried to Java via Australia. They would be followed by P-40s sent to Java from Australia to protect this bomber force.

A second shipment of 55 P-40Es was delivered to Brisbane aboard the SS *Polk* on 15 January, followed by a third shipment of 67 P-40Es via the SS *Mormacsun* on 21 January. On 2 February the *Mariposa* and *Coolidge* delivered a further 57 airframes, 27 of which were reloaded on the *Sea Witch* for direct shipment to Java. Meanwhile another 32 Warhawks had been flown across to Freemantle in Western Australia where they were loaded onto the old carrier USS *Langley*. However, this ship was sunk on approach to Java on 27 February.

Meanwhile at Amberley some "provisional" USAAC pursuit squadrons had been hurriedly formed. These departed at separate times on a long ferry route across the Australian outback to Darwin, and then via a southern NEI island route to Java.

This first of the new units was designated the 17th PS (Provisional) and was formed on 14 January 1942 under Major Charles Sprague. Experienced pilots evacuated from the Philippines swelled the squadron's ranks to seventeen pilots. The P-40Es left Amberley in two flights, the first of nine led by a twin-engine Beechcraft 18, whilst a second of eight was led by two RAAF Fairey Battles. All arrived safely at the first leg, Rockhampton, however *en route* Lieutenant Carl Geiss crashed box #6 sidelining it from delivery. The others proceeded to Townsville to overnight where box #14 was damaged on landing. The following day, the others made their way to Cloncurry then Daly Waters where yet another P-40E was damaged. On 19 January 1942, they then waited at Darwin several days pending engineering support delivered by RAAF DC-2s. Finally, they departed for Java on 25 January and shortly thereafter entered combat, their markings falling outside of this volume.

The 17th PS (Provisional) was followed to Java by the 3rd and 20th PS (Provisional) in subsequent weeks, although these later two units suffered significant attrition along the way. The surviving aircraft and their pilots were merged into the 17th PS (Provisional) when they arrived in Java.

Two other squadrons, the 13th and 33rd PS (Provisional), had the most junior pilots and were involved in a rushed plan to load aircraft on the *Langley* at Freemantle as mentioned above. However, halfway to Western Australia most of the 33rd PS (Provisional) under Major Floyd Pell was ordered north to Darwin to protect an important convoy. Pell's redirected flight tracked the railway line to Alice Springs in central Australia before reaching Darwin via Daly Waters. On take-off from Daly Waters, Lieutenant Robert McMahon's *Bahootee the Cootee* struck a tractor near the runway, damaging his undercarriage, but he nonetheless reached Darwin, as described below.

Aside from Lieutenant Richard Suers who force-landed along the way, all of other Warhawks had arrived at Darwin by late afternoon of 15 February, joining a sole airworthy P-40E of the 3rd PS (Provisional) flown by Lieutenant Robert Oestreicher. McMahon's undercarriage collapsed on landing at Darwin, and thus he abandoned the original *Bahootee the Cootee* (box #29).

Box 261 was P-40E serial 41-5626, and is seen at Laverton, Victoria, in February 1942.

The art on the port fuselage of Bahootee the Cootee No. II (the subject of Profile 2) shortly after McMahon force-landed it near Darwin on 17 February 1942.

The starboard side of Profile 2 showing the name Mac following its force-landing of 17 February 1942.

PACIFIC PROFILES

Early Warhawks

Profile 1: P-40E serial unknown, squadron #14, *J.C Penny-Lou*, 17th PS (Provisional)

This P-40E was delivered to Java by 17th PS (Provisional) commander Major Charles Sprague. It was maintained and named by crew chief Master Sergeant Lynman Goltry after his girlfriend who worked in a San Rafael chain store. It was the first shark-mouth Warhawk in Australia, decorated by Second Lieutenant Joseph Kruzel.

Profile 2: P-40E serial unknown, *Mac / Bahootee the Cootee No. II*, 33rd PS (Provisional)

When Lieutenant Robert McMahon took delivery of this second Warhawk the red circle inside the national insignia had already been reduced by the original 3rd PS (Provisional) pilot. It had been left in Darwin on 10 February 1942 after 3rd PS (Provisional) pilot Second Lieutenant George Kiser ferried it there. McMahon named his replacement Warhawk *Bahootee the Cootee No. II* and also painted *Mac*, his nickname, on the starboard side. McMahon force-landed this airframe at Darwin on 17 February 1942 when the engine failed. McMahon was issued another replacement, P-40E box #22, which he named *Bahootee the Cootee No. III*. However, he baled out of it when shot down by Zeros during the 19 February carrier strike against Darwin.

Profile 3: P-40E-1 serial 41-36231, ET877

This Warhawk is profiled as it came out of its packing box at either RAAF Laverton or Richmond in late April 1942 from New Orleans, with a temperate camouflage scheme and white spinner. It was diverted to Australia for the RAAF from a shipment originally intended for Britain. Whilst its box contained stencils for British insignia, these were not used and USAAC roundels were later painted on at the Replacement Pool at Charleville *en route* to delivery to the 49th FG at Darwin.

Profile 4: P-40E serial unknown, box #54, 3rd PS (Provisional)

Lieutenant Robert Buel and Robert Oestreicher were stranded in Darwin with two unserviceable P-40Es when the rest of the 3rd PS departed for Java on 10 February 1942. On 15 February the USS *Houston* broke radio silence to advise it was being shadowed by an enemy flying boat. This was one of three Toko *Ku* H6K4 Mavis based at Ceram conducting extended patrols. The Mavis shadowed the convoy for about three hours before it dropped 60-kilogram bombs from 10,000 feet. Both Buel and Oestreicher were on patrol in the area but only Buel responded to a Darwin radio call to intercept the flying boat. He attacked it from the rear but was shot down by the tail gunner firing a 20mm cannon. However, the Mavis was also shot down, with the surviving crew reaching an island north of Darwin where they became POWs.

Profile 5: P-40E serial 41-5456, box #36, *Dumbo*, 33rd PS (Provisional)

Second Lieutenant John Glover scrambled to get airborne in this fighter from RAAF Darwin during the 19 February 1942 carrier strike. He crashed after hitting a tree during take-off, and then witnessed his wrecked aircraft being strafed by Japanese Zeros. Glover's injuries warranted him medical evacuation on the hospital ship *Manunda* the following day. Despite its name, the artwork is actually that of a goose with dark under feathers firing a machine gun.

P-40E 36, the subject of Profile 9, at Darwin for a publicity photo-shoot. Many of the Warhawks in this line-up were spruced up and decorated for the occasion.

CHAPTER 3
7th Fighter Squadron "Screamin' Demons"

Note: this chapter also contains some associated history of the 49th PG/FG, relevant also to the 8th and 9th PS/FS.

This squadron was one of three to arise from the creation of the 49th Pursuit Group, formed in the US in late 1941 from a pilot cadre transferred from the 94th PG.[1] At inception, its pilots trained on the PT-17 Stearman, the PT-13 Basic Trainer for instrument flying and three Seversky P-35s. A solitary P-40C served as the sole modern fighter for combat training. Its three squadrons, the 7th, 8th and 9th Pursuit Squadrons later took the names *Screamin' Demons*, *Black Sheep* and *Flying Knights*. On 16 May 1941 the group moved via truck convoy to its new base at Morrison airfield near West Palm Beach.

Major Paul Wurtsmith took over command of the 49th PG on 12 December 1941, and held the position for about a year until replaced in turn by Lieutenant Colonel Donald Hutchinson, Lieutenant Colonel Robert Morrissey and then Colonel James Selman from 30 July 1943. Wurtsmith later became the youngest USAAF general when he led Fifth Air Force Fighter Command.

When it departed the US in early January 1942, the 49th PG was initially bound for the Philippines. However, following the US retreat to Bataan, the ship's destination was changed mid-voyage to Melbourne, where it docked on 1 February. There the 7th PS was reassigned a coterie of experienced pilots who had survived the Philippines campaign. These included Captain Nate Blanton, Captain Bill Hennon and Lieutenant Lester Johnson, all of whom became flight leaders. On 22 February, Captains Robert Morrissey, Robert Van Auken and James Selman were appointed commanders of the 7th, 8th and 9th Pursuit Squadrons respectively. Soon the home of the 7th PS, Bankstown aerodrome and the associated squadron camp, was termed "Yank town" by the locals. The aerodrome was also used as a ferry destination and collection place for the group's other two squadrons, when their just-assembled Warhawks were ferried down from Amberley or Geelong, Victoria.

An understanding of the immediate high attrition of airframes helps understand why so much markings complexity ensued with the 49th PG, even from the outset. The 7th PS had its first accident on its first day of operations, when Second Lieutenant Frederick O'Riley tore up a section of fence before crashing into the kitchen of a civilian house two miles west of Bankstown. The P-40E was damaged beyond repair, but O'Riley merely received a lip injury, and the occupants of the house were unharmed.

This was followed by three more accidents on 25 February. Second Lieutenant Oliver Vodrey

---

[1] The USAAC became the USAAF in March 1942. Two months later the Pursuit Groups and Pursuit Squadrons were redesignated as Fighter Groups and Fighter Squadrons.

force landed near Wyong, New South Wales, and after his fighter overturned one of his fingers was partially amputated. The P-40 was dismantled and trucked back to Bankstown. Second Lieutenant Clarence Wilmarth's left maingear wheel collapsed on landing at Bankstown and Second Lieutenant Warren Jackson force landed at Laugh Park near the West Maitland showgrounds. He received an upper fractured jaw and was taken to West Maitland Hospital.

On 26 February a 25-ship composite 7th and 9th PS formation was ferried up to Archerfield aerodrome near Brisbane. On landing one 9th PS Warhawk flown by Second Lieutenant Edward Ball was damaged when he taxied into an anti-aircraft gun position. The following day, whilst practicing landings at Camden after taking off from Bankstown, Second Lieutenant James Archerbald's 7th PS #15 veered off the runway and collided with a car, before crashing into a hangar. That same afternoon Second Lieutenant John Fisher overturned on landing at Bankstown.

During this early period, several RAAF Kittyhawk pilots were attached to the unit to assist in training. They utilised two seat Wirraways for dual instruction, with a focus on training the numerous low-hour USAAC graduate pilots assigned to all three squadrons. Nonetheless yet another 7th PS accident happened on 1 March when Second Lieutenant Austin Holly force-landed on the hillside overlooking Bankstown, destroying the Warhawk.

On 4 March Morrissey led eleven Warhawks from Bankstown for a brief deployment to Horn Island at Australia's northern tip, in order to safeguard the Port Moresby air delivery route. With no engineering facilities along the route, each pilot was issued with a basic tool kit including spare spark plugs. The armorers trained the pilots how to load the wing machine guns, and Morrissey carried a wobble pump/hose kit with which to refuel from stockpiled fuel drums. Maritime maps were carried to navigate the Queensland littoral, however three Warhawks diverted to Charters Towers *en route* with mechanical problems. The remaining eight landed at Horn Island on the afternoon of 8 March, commencing patrols the next day. Meanwhile the 9th PS had advanced to Darwin later that same month, whilst the 8th PS based itself at RAAF Fairbairn near Canberra, Australia's capital, where it was held in reserve pending strategic developments. On 8 April it too arrived at Darwin, where the entire 49th FG spent several months fighting off Japanese raids.

On 11 November 1942, "Squeeze" Wurtsmith handed over command of the 49th FG to Lieutenant Colonel Donald Hutchinson, after which the group's three squadrons proceeded to New Guinea and set up camp at Port Moresby. In preparation for the move the Warhawks of the 7th and 8th FS had been ferried from Darwin to Townsville in September 1942.

As was usual for any USAAF unit moving to a new theatre, non-combat losses were the rule and not the exception. The 7th FS suffered several such losses when it first arrived at Schwimmer 'drome, Port Moresby, with the first happening on 28 September resulting in a forced-landing near Hood Point from fuel starvation. The next non-combat loss occurred on 2 November when Second Lieutenant Bryant Wesley ditched in Bootless Bay following an engine failure (as noted in Profile 6). Then, on 17 November First Lieutenant William Hanning got lost in bad weather when returning from escorting RAAF Beaufighters to Lae. He too ran out of fuel but safely force-landed near Hula village on the southern coast.

The 7th FS moved operations from Port Moresby to Dobodura on 15 April 1943, then to Gusap on 16 November 1943, Finschhafen on 27 April 1944 and then it left the main New Guinea theatre when it moved to Hollandia on 3 May 1944. It converted to P-38s later that same year. The squadron lost 27 Warhawks to non-combat causes in the Australian and New Guinea theatres, including from oxygen failures, engine failures, losses to bad weather and two airframes lost in two separate mid-air collisions. The unit lost a further 17 Warhawks to combat.

Squadron Markings

The "box number" described in Chapter 1 originally appeared on the fins of most 49th FG P-40Es and P-40E-1s when unpacked. This has led to aircraft misidentification when mistaken for individual "buzz" or squadron numbers, or even part of a serial number. Squadron numbers were allocated to the group's Warhawks in the following sequence: 1-9 for the Headquarters Flight, 10-39 for the 7th FS, 40-69 for the 8th FS and 70-99 for the 9th FS. Some "box numbers" remained extant throughout their combat service, although in most cases they were painted over. This factor has also confused markings interpretations.

The 7th FS logo features a bunyip, a fictitious Australian creature which allegedly resides in billabongs (geographically isolated river sections). The creature continues to be referred to erroneously in US circles as a "bunyap", the term used by the squadron incumbents.

Second Lieutenant Arthur T House sits atop Hero's Poopy, the subject of Profile 7.

PACIFIC PROFILES

7th Fighter Squadron

Profile 6: P-40E serial 41-5313, squadron number 13, *Poopey*

Flight leader Second Lieutenant Arthur T House, Jr was universally nicknamed "AT" for his initials. On 14 March 1942 he departed from Horn Island in this assigned Warhawk as one of four P-40Es led by Captain Bob Morrissey. They were intent on intercepting a combined formation of No. 4 *Ku* Zeros and Bettys, however during the ensuing dogfight around midday, House discovered his guns were inoperative. He impulsively rammed a Zero which was closely pursuing other Warhawks. The Zero (tail code F-114), exploded and spiraled into the ocean.

House managed to land his badly damaged Warhawk at Horn Island on the third approach. Despite its extensive structural damage, the airframe was later ferried to a service depot where it was overhauled and placed back in squadron service. On 2 November 1942, following the squadron's move to New Guinea, Second Lieutenant Bryant Wesley ditched the fighter in Bootless Bay near Port Moresby following an engine failure. The fighter is illustrated as it appeared on 14 March, with a yellow vertical stripe indicating House's flight leader status and wheel hubs decorated with red dots. Note that grey paint had already been applied over the inner red circle of the national insignia prior to the relevant USAAC orders. Box number 303 remained extant on the fin.

Profile 7: P-40E serial unknown, squadron number 13, *Hero's Poopy*

Following House's collision described in Profile 6, he named his next assigned P-40E *Hero's Poopy* (without an "e") in response to the good-natured ribbing he received for downing a Zero by collision. Later, in early 1943 he was assigned P-40K serial 42-46288 which he named *Poopey II* and which also was allocated squadron number 13. As with Profile 6, the yellow vertical stripe indicates flight leader status.

Profile 8: P-40E serial unknown, squadron number 32

This Warhawk was destroyed in a take-off accident on 29 April 1942 when Lieutenant JW Tyler crashed into a Lockheed C-40 transport at Batchelor, south of Darwin. Tyler suffered only minor injuries, but the crash killed General Hal George and journalist Melvin Jacoby.

Profile 9: P-40E serial unknown, squadron number 36

This early P-40E was assigned to Captain Bill Hennon at Darwin in April 1942. The figure on the rudder is a developed version of the squadron's "bunyip" insignia. The white fuselage band denotes Hennon as a flight leader. Note the white decorative flying wheel applied on the red hub cap.

Profile 10: P-40E serial 41-5553, squadron number 11, *Jeanne*

Jeanne was assigned to Major George Prentice who later in the war was appointed the first commanding officer of the elite 475th FG. The artwork on the rudder is a cartoon devil superimposed against a yellow sun to the left. This cartoon was an early adaptation of the squadron's "bunyip" insignia, as described above. The painted-over black stencil 204 on the fin was the aircraft's box number. This early P-40 is profiled as it appeared at Batchelor field in the Northern Territory in late March 1942. On 2 June 1942 Lieutenant Oliver Vodrey had an accident in the aircraft at Batchelor and, although officially condemned on paper, it was in fact repaired and placed back into service with the 7th FS.

PACIFIC PROFILES

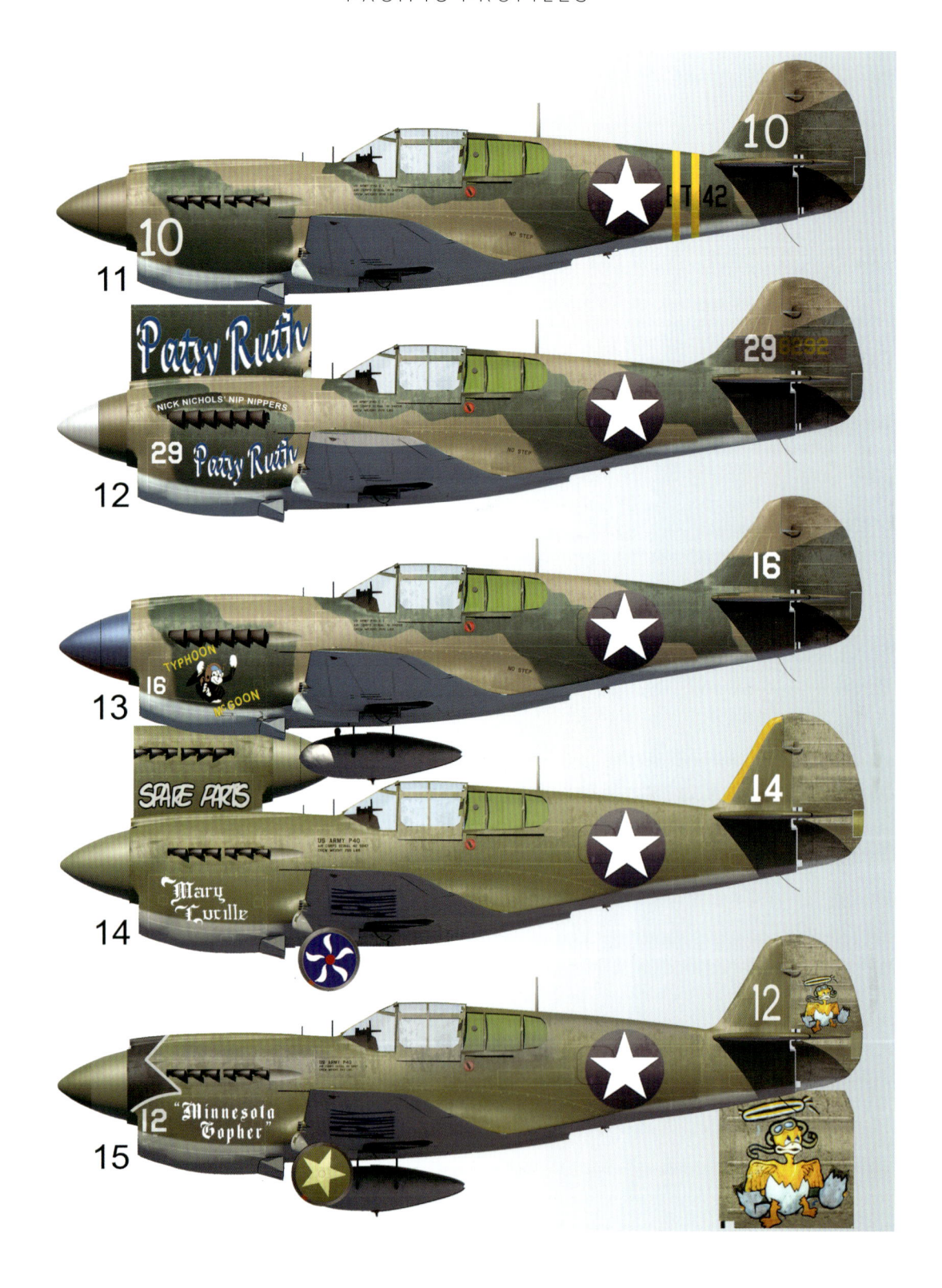

PAGE 34

Profile 11: P-40E-1 serial 41-24818, British serial ET142, squadron number 10

This early P-40E-1 was first assigned to 7th PS commander Captain Bob Morrissey who had the double vertical yellow stripes to identify his position. It was damaged on 4 May 1942, but was rebuilt as a P-40E and reassigned as squadron number 37 with the 8th FS in mid-August 1942 along with eight other Warhawks which had been classified as write-offs. Such renovations were colloquially termed "refits" in USAAF terminology. In turn it was transferred on 7 September 1942 to the RAAF.

Profile 12: P-40K-1 serial 42-46292, squadron number 29, *Patsy Ruth*

Patsy Ruth was assigned to First Lieutenant Arland Stanton at 30-Mile (Rorona) 'drome in December 1942, just before the 7th FS relocated to Schwimmer 'drome, Port Moresby. Captain Frank Nichols named his Red Flight *Nick Nichol's Nip Nippers*, and *Patsy Ruth* was one of several in the flight which stencilled this title above the cowl in white. The fighter took hits over Wau on 6 February 1943, during combat with Ki-48 Lily light bombers and Ki-43 Oscars. *Patsy Ruth* is profiled as it first appeared at Rorona, before Stanton applied bomb and two kill markings. In late February 1943, *Patsy Ruth*'s spinner was repainted red, the Flight's colour, and nose number 29 was repainted slightly larger in yellow.

Profile 13: P-40K-5 serial 42-46285, squadron number 16, *Typhoon McGoon*

Named by First Lieutenant Clyde Knisley, this K model was flown throughout the 1943 New Guinea campaign. When the 7th FS started upgrading to N models this airframe was returned to the US on 4 April 1944 where it briefly served as a trainer.

Profile 14: P-40E-1 serial 41-24868 (P-40E refit), British serial ET192, squadron number 14, *Mary Lucille*

Delivered to Brisbane in February 1942, this P-40E was quickly assigned to the 7th FS. It was allocated to Second Lieutenant Joseph King on 6 March 1942 who named the fighter *Mary Lucille* after his wife. Originally assigned squadron number 31, King flew *Mary Lucille* throughout much of the 1942 Darwin campaign before the fighter was refitted as a P-40E, painted in Olive Drab and allocated squadron number 14. Pilot Second Lieutenant Larry Hansen took it for a test flight from Batchelor on 24 August 1942, but its engine seized and Hansen baled out. The aircraft is portrayed as it appeared the day it was lost in its refit scheme. *Spare Parts* was painted on the cowl's starboard side to commemorate the numerous modifications made during the refit. The yellow fin leading edge was a marking from the 7th FS's later Darwin era.

Profile 15: P-40E serial 41-5449, squadron number 12, *Minnesota Gopher*

Delivered to Australia on 30 January 1942 in box #157, on 13 June 1942 this Warhawk bellied in four miles from Daly Waters near a river following an engine failure. It was flown by Second Lieutenant Harold "Hal" Martin from Minnesota who named and decorated the fighter including the star on the wheel hubs. Following repairs it was transferred to the RAAF. The art on the rudder depicted a fledgling aviator duck recently hatched.

PACIFIC PROFILES

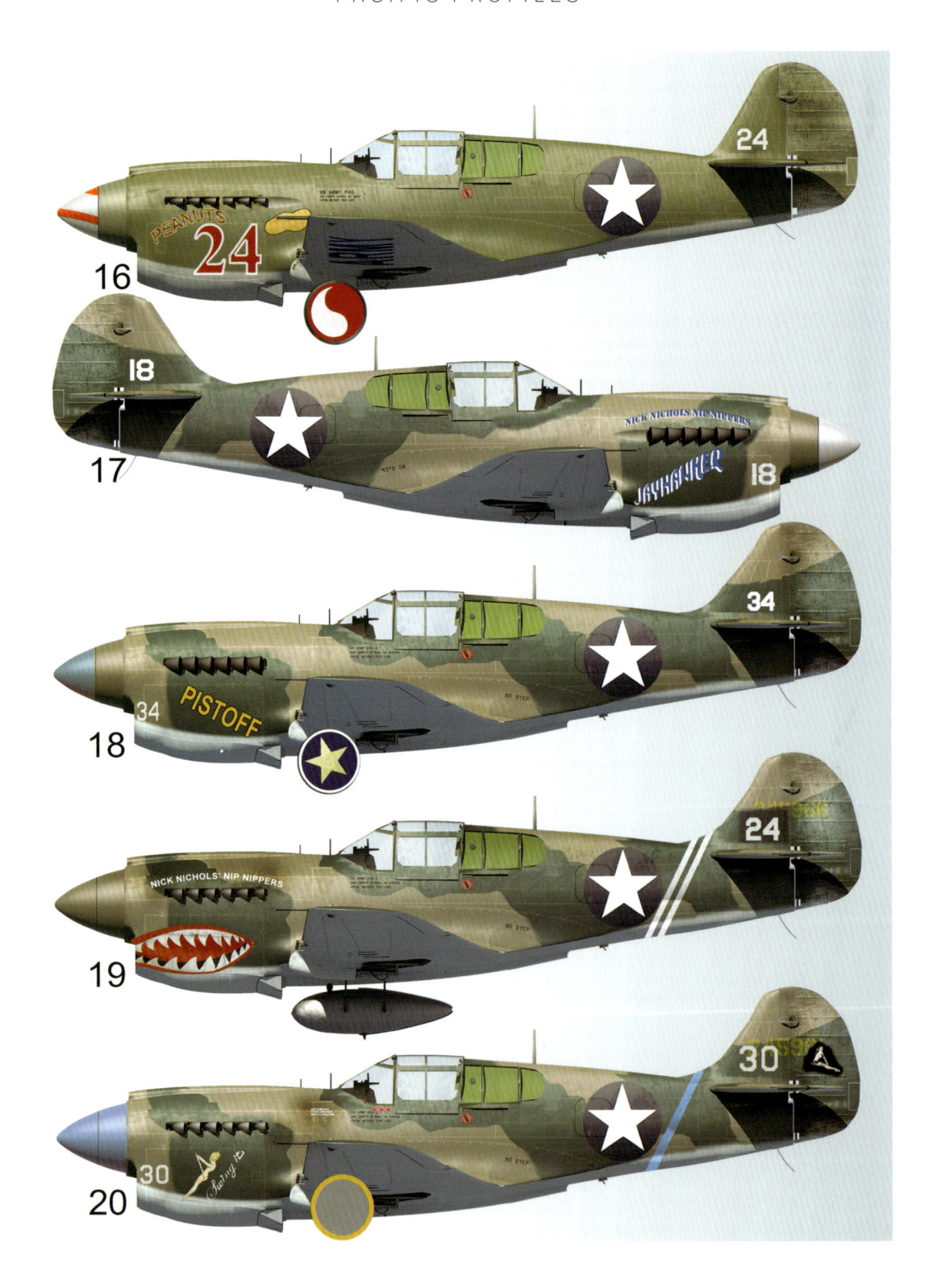

PAGE 36

Profile 16: P-40E serial unknown, squadron number 24, *Peanuts*

This early P-40E served throughout the Darwin campaign flown mainly by Lieutenant Lester "Les" Johnson who named the aircraft as a self-depreciating gesture to indicate his fighter's worth. Note the spirals on the spinner and the red and white "Yin and Yang" wheel hub.

Profile 17: P-40K-1 serial 42-46276, squadron number 18, *Jayhawker*

This K model was named *Jayhawker* by First Lieutenant David Allen who flew it mainly in New Guinea. The other side of the cowl was named *Gloria*. As a member of Red Flight and similar to Profile 12, *Jayhawker* was one of several Warhawks which had stenciled *Nick Nichol's Nip Nippers* above the exhaust stack. On 3 July 1943 First Lieutenant Carl Aubrey was flying this fighter when he made his only combat claim – a Ki-43-II Oscar fighter in the Salus Lake Area along the northern New Guinea coast, just south of Lae. The airframe was returned to the US in 1944 where it served briefly as a trainer.

Profile 18: P-40K-1 serial 42-45979, squadron number 34, *Pistoff*

This fighter was a replacement to the original number 34, a similarly named P-40E lost at Batchelor on 2 June 1942 while landing in dusty conditions. Flying this fighter First Lieutenant Donald Lee claimed a Ki-43-II Oscar over Lae during the Battle of the Bismarck Sea on 5 March 1943, however on 14 July 1943 return fire from a D3A2 Val dive bomber hit the engine's Prestone coolant pipes. After the engine shut down Lee ditched near Salamaua and was rescued by torpedo boat PT-150. *Pistoff* is illustrated just prior to its loss when it was based at Dobodura.

Profile 19: P-40K-1 serial 42-45966, squadron number 24, *Nick Nichol's Nip Nippers*

This fighter was assigned to Red Flight leader, Captain Frank Nichols, and named *Nick Nichol's Nip Nippers* as per Profiles 12 and 17. He made his second claim near Buna on 7 December 1942 when flying this fighter, however it was later lost in a landing accident at Dobodura on 18 June 1943. This Warhawk was one of the few to carry a shark-mouth, and the two white stripes denoted Nichol's status as the 7th FS Operations Officer.

Profile 20 : P-40K-1 serial 42-45984, squadron number 30, *Swing It*

This airframe was unpacked from its crate in Australia on 19 August 1942 before delivery to the 7th FS in October. It was placed in the hands of Captain Ray Melikan. The blue slanted stripe indicated Melikan's status as the leader of blue flight, and the girl on the rope swing was a direct copy from an Alberto Vargas calendar. Three Japanese flags indicate Melikan's victory claims of 30 July 1942, 23 August 1942 and 5 March 1943. In mid-December 1942, fledgling pilot Second Lieutenant Harry Dillworth badly damaged the fighter during a landing accident at 14-Mile 'drome, Port Moresby. The rear of the airframe was bent; however, it was repaired to airworthy status. The fighter is profiled as it appeared around this time, including grey wheel hubs with a yellow border. The fighter was lost on 27 April 1943 about five miles north of Popondetta when Second Lieutenant Chris Props dropped from formation at 18,000 feet and entered a spin, likely due to oxygen failure. In September 1946 his incomplete remains were recovered.

PACIFIC PROFILES

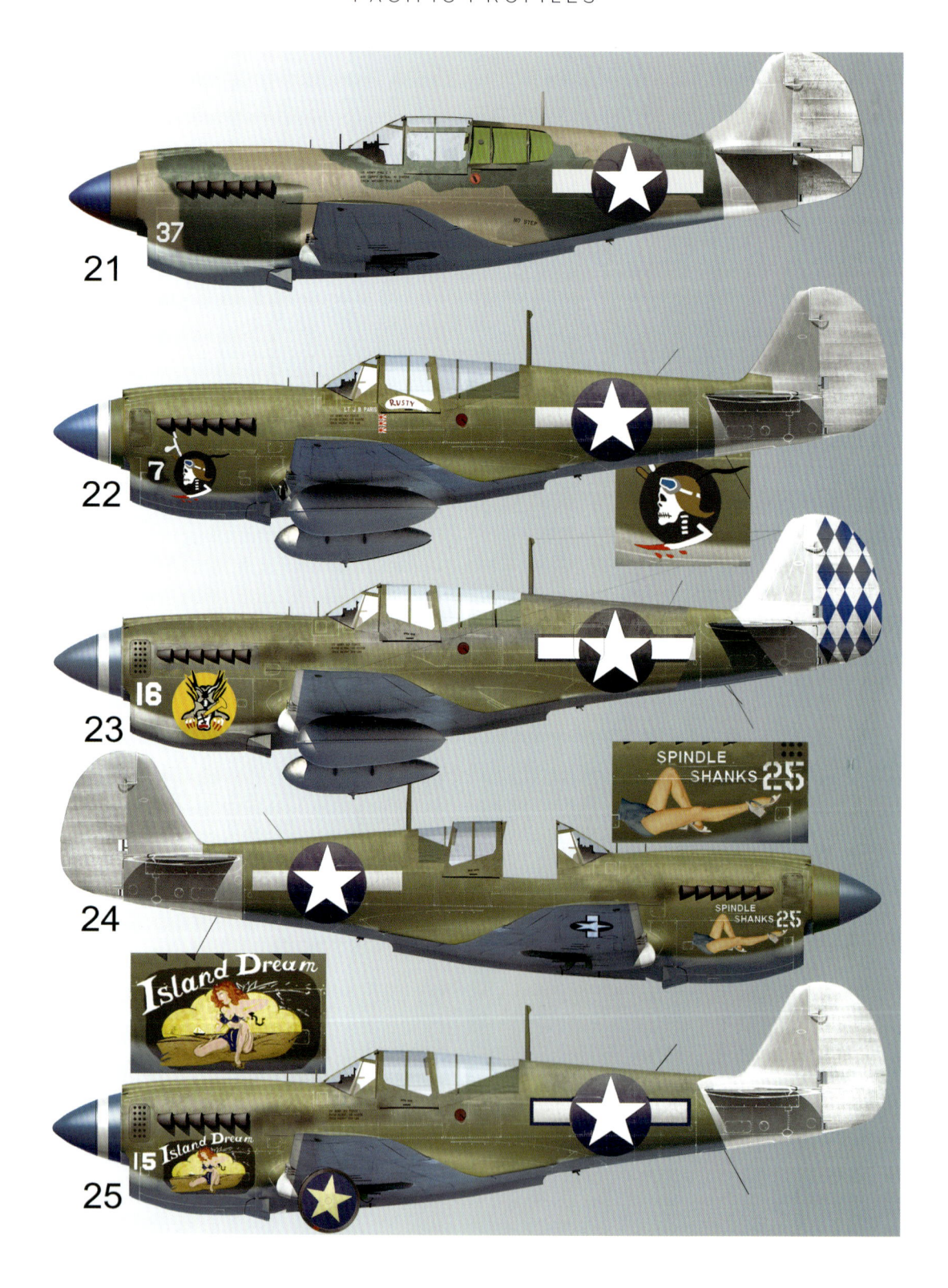

21

22

23

24

25

Profile 21 : P-40K-1 serial unknown, squadron number 37

This Warhawk was one of the few K models which had white tail markings applied in the theatre from late August 1943 onwards. It was assigned to Lieutenant Ray Hillard and was one of the last K models to see service at Dobodura well into 1943.

Profile 22 : P-40N-5 serial unknown, squadron number 7, *Rusty*

This airframe is often misrepresented in a camouflage scheme, which no N model had in theatre. It was assigned to Lieutenant Joel Paris who named and decorated it. The airframe is illustrated as it appeared at Finschhafen in late 1943 by which time its wings had been fitted with extra hard points to carry wing-mounted drop tanks. Note that as a result of installation of a bypass carburetor intake the previous holed panel intake has been replaced.

Profile 23: P-40N-20 serial unknown, squadron number 16,

Captain Nathaniel Blanton had the bunyip logo painted on the front cowl, along with a blue chequered tail. This late model Warhawk was assigned to the 7th FS at New Guinea around March 1944.

Profile 24: P-40N-20 serial unknown, squadron number 25, *Spindle Shanks*

Lieutenant Gene "Ben" Pollock was the regular pilot of squadron number 25. On the port cowl he painted the name *Lovely Lavinia* after a girlfriend back home. Note that, similar to Profile 22, the bypass carburetor panel intake just behind the spinner has been replaced with a solid cover. On 12 March 1944, Pollock was credited with one enemy fighter when flying this Warhawk over Brandi Plantation near Wewak.

Profile 25 : P-40N-5 serial 42-105202, squadron number 15, *Island Dream*

The nose art on Captain Roger Farrell's mount exemplifies the 7th FS's new style of lascivious art which began appearing towards its final weeks in New Guinea in mid-1944. It was later transferred to the 110th Tactical Reconnaissance Squadron.

P-40N-5 42-105202 Island Dream, as depicted in Profile 25, shortly after receipt of its artwork including decorated hubs.

A 7th FS P-40 takes-off from an airfield south of Darwin in 1942.

P-40E serial 41-5553 Jeanne, the subject of Profile 10, at a northern Australian airfield.

P-40K-1 serial 42-45984 Swing It, the subject of Profile 20, in New Guinea prior to the addition of the third Japanese flag indicating a kill on 5 March 1943.

P-40K-1 serial 42-45979 Pistoff, the subject of Profile 18, at Port Moresby's 17-Mile 'drome

P-40N-20 Spindle Shanks, as depicted in Profile 24, at Gusap in New Guinea's Ramu Valley.

P-40N-20 squadron number 16 with the bunyip artwork as depicted in Profile 23.

P-40K-1 serial 42-46276 Jayhawker, as depicted in Profile 17, at Dobodura. Note Nick Nichol's Nip Nippers stenciled above the exhaust stack.

P-40N-5 Rusty, as shown in Profile 22, at Finschhafen in late 1943. Note the bat on the forward undercarriage housing.

P-40E serial 41-5455, as depicted in Profile 26, following its force-landing near Eden in New South Wales on 28 March 1942.

The underside of P-40E serial 41-5455 (Profile 26) after the aircraft was dismantled following a forced landing on a beach. This view which showcases the dark blue underwing US ARMY stencils.

CHAPTER 4
8th Fighter Squadron "The Blacksheep"

The 8th PS was one of the three squadrons which comprised the 49th FG formed in the US in late 1941. It later took the name *The Blacksheep*. The unit docked in Melbourne on 1 February, led by Lieutenant Robert Van Auken. When all three of the 49th PG's squadrons received several experienced pilots who had survived the Philippines and Java campaigns, the 8th PS was allocated flight leaders Captain Allison Strauss and First Lieutenant George Kiser, along with Lieutenants RC Docksteder and Jim Morehead as element leaders. Strauss soon replaced Van Auken as squadron commander but was killed during combat over Darwin on 27 April 1942. His replacement was Captain "Eck" Mitchell Sims. Following months of combat defending Darwin, the 8th FS left the theatre and moved to Townsville. It later ferried its Warhawks to Port Moresby, New Guinea, on 25 September 1942 from where it flew its first combat mission on 1 November 1942.

It moved to Dobodura on 15 April 1943, then to Tsili Tsili on 30 August 1943 in preparation for the invasion of Lae. It relocated to Gusap on 29 October 1943 and left the main New Guinea theatre when it moved Hollandia on 3 May 1944. In late August that same year the squadron commenced conversion to the P-38 Lightning. The 8th FS lost 31 Warhawks to non-combat causes in the Australian and New Guinea theatres, including to take-off and landing accidents, one mid-air collision, engine failures and several losses to bad weather. It lost 18 Warhawks directly to combat.

Squadron Markings

Squadron numbers 40-69 were allocated to the 8th FS Warhawks. Similar to the 49th FG's other two squadrons, "box numbers" remained extant on many early P-40E airframes throughout their service, confusing markings interpretations. The spinners on the P-40Ns appeared in different designs of yellow, the squadron colour.

P-40E serial 41-5543 Smiley, as shown in Profile 29, under a camouflage net at Darwin in May 1942.

PACIFIC PROFILES

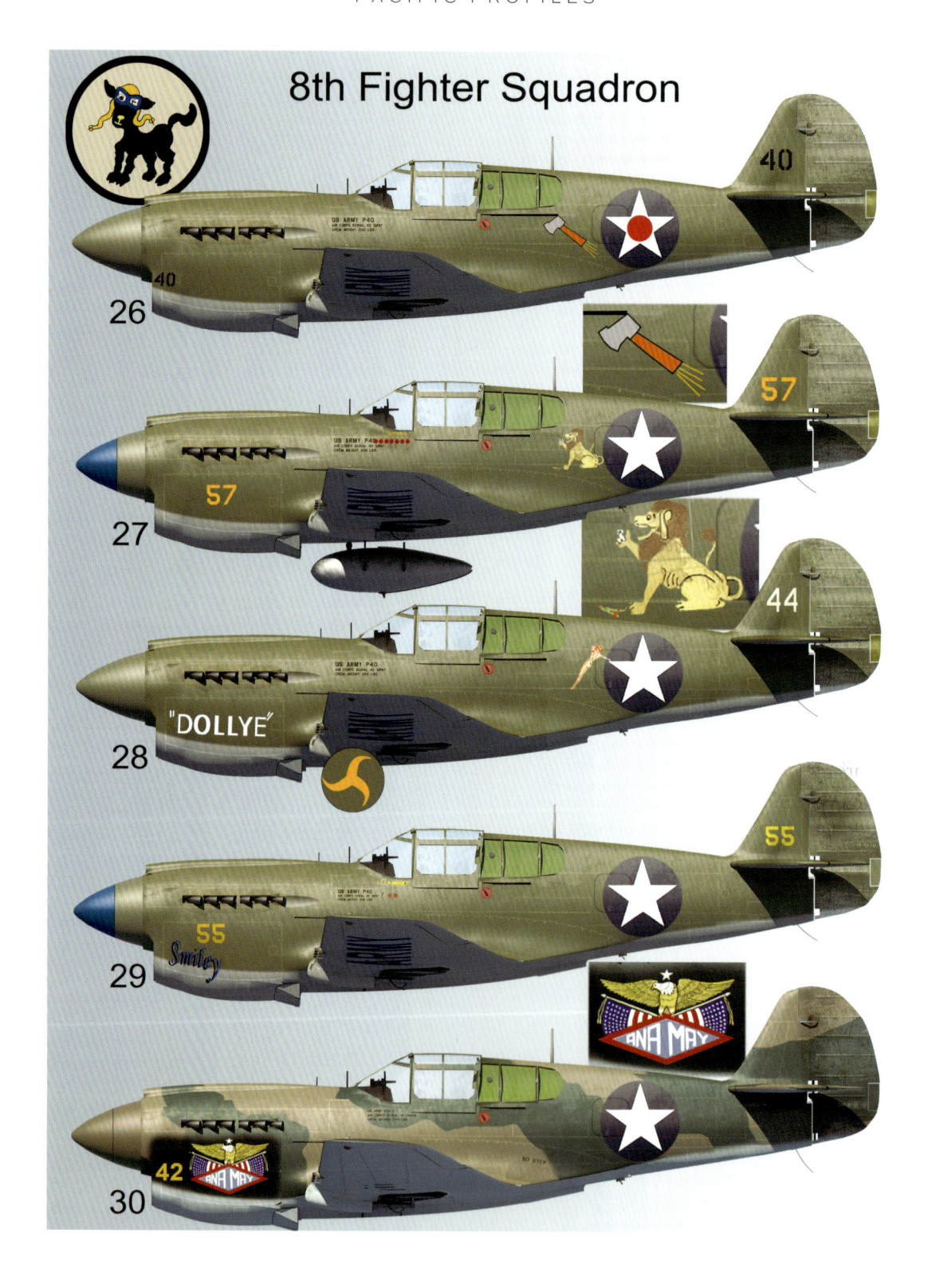

8th Fighter Squadron

26

27

28 "DOLLYE"

29 Smiley

30 ANA MAY

PAGE 46

Profile 26 – P-40E serial 41-5455, squadron number 40, (flying axe)

Lieutenant Arthur "Doc" Fielder force-landed this Warhawk uninjured on Aslings Beach near Eden in New South Wales on 28 March 1942 during a routine training flight. Fielder was one of four pilots from Canberra that day who became disorientated in poor visibility. Lieutenants Neil Takala and John Musial were both killed when their fighters crashed in mountainous terrain behind Eden. Meanwhile, Fielder's P-40E was first taken by barge across Twofold Bay to Boydtown Beach where an attempted take-off was unsuccessful. It was then dismantled and transported to RAAF Fairbairn by truck. Fielder was later killed during a training flight at Strauss airfield in the Northern Territory on 23 June 1942.

Profile 27 – P-40E serial 41-5622, squadron number 57, (lion)

This P-40E was serving with the 7th FS when it was one of several photographed for publicity purposes at RAAF Darwin in April 1942. It was then reassigned to Captain George Kiser of the 8th FS. Kiser had previously served as a B-17 pilot in Java but had retrained on fighters. All four P-40s in Kiser's Blue Flight had the front half of their spinner painted blue. Kiser's gunnery skills were well-honed, and he removed the two outer 0.50-inch calibre machine guns from the wings thus increasing the amount of ammunition for the remaining four. He told fellow pilots this initiative gave him a better chance to maintain combat with Zeros in an extended fight. The fighter is profiled with seven red circles indicating seven claimed victories. Kiser decorated the rear fuselage with a lion motif, whose left paw held down a Zero, whilst its right one places a Japanese aviator in its mouth.

Profile 28 – P-40E serial 40-681, squadron number 44, *Dollye*

On 13 June 1942 this early P-40E was badly shot up in combat by Zeros. Pilot Lieutenant Monroe "Monty" Eisenberg ground-looped the aircraft at Livingstone field during landing, and it flipped over on its back. The airframe was placed back into squadron service following extensive repairs as per Profile 37. Eisenberg received a replacement fighter which he named *Dollye 2nd* and left the theatre after he flew his last combat mission on 26 August 1942. The fighter is illustrated the way it appeared on the date of its 13 June accident.

Profile 29 – P-40E serial 41-5543, squadron number 55, *Smiley* (port cowl)

Smiley was the nickname given to Captain George Kiser's wingman, Second Lieutenant Clyde Barnett. The fighter was included in Kiser's Blue Flight at Darwin and was one of the four Warhawks in this flight which had the front half of its spinner painted blue. The fighter is profiled with two red circles indicating two claimed victories. The fighter was lost on 7 June 1942 when Second Lieutenant Harvey Martin ditched it in surf on the southern shore of Melville Island.

Profile 30 – P-40E-1 serial unknown, squadron number 42, *Ana May*

Lieutenant Nelson Flack was assigned this war-weary P-40E-1 at Dobodura when he joined the 8th FS at Dobodura in May 1943. From Pennsylvania, Flack learned to fly with the Royal Canadian Air Force. The lavish art, including golden eagle and patriotic colours, was painted over a previous unidentified name, hence the dark backdrop. Flack only flew the aircraft briefly before it was replaced with a P-40N.

PACIFIC PROFILES

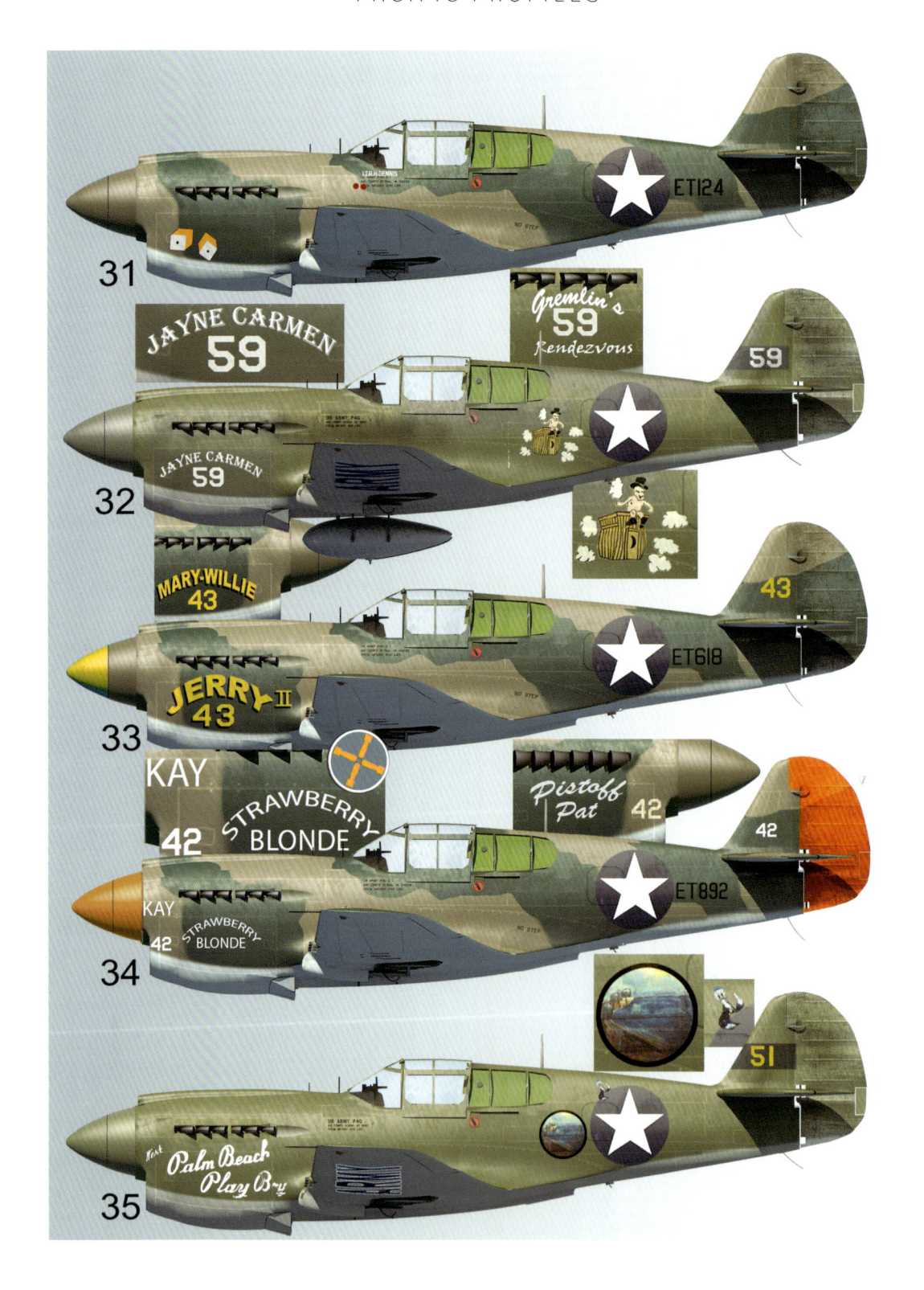

PAGE 48

Profile 31 – Curtiss P-40E-1 serial 41-24800, British serial ET124, *Craps*

This P-40E-1 was in the first batch assigned to the 8th FS on 8 March 1942. On 18 December 1942 it went missing in the New Guinea mountains near Kokoda flown by First Lieutenant Richard Dennis. The fighter was one of four which departed Port Moresby at 1255 to patrol the Cape Ward Hunt area on the northern coastline. About half an hour before the patrol was due to end, Dennis broke away from the formation and headed south back towards base. The others followed but he again broke off to the left and that was the last time he was seen. The two red circles were victory markers from two combat claims over Darwin.

Profile 32 – Curtiss P-40E serial 41-5648, squadron number 59, *Jayne Carmen / Gremlin's Rendezvous*

This Warhawk was initially assigned to 8th FS commander Captain "Eck" Mitchell Sims at Darwin who crash-landed it at the emergency field at Adelaide River on 2 August 1942 following combat. Sims applied the quirky art of a naked cartoon character sitting on a crude Australian outhouse. It was repaired and went to New Guinea with the squadron in late 1942. There it was reassigned to Robert Howard who renamed it after his girlfriend who he married after the war.

Profile 33 – Curtiss P-40E-1 serial 41-35972, British serial ET-618, squadron number 43, *Jerry II / Mary-Willie*

This airframe was assigned to Lieutenant William Day at Horanda 'drome in early 1943. His first *Jerry* was an unidentified P-40, also squadron number 43, which was flown from Darwin. It was subsequently lost to operations or combat when based at Port Moresby. *Jerry II* is profiled as it appeared at Horanda 'drome. It eventually became a trainer before it was decommissioned as war weary. The name *Mary-Willie* on the starboard cowl was applied by the fighter's crew chief.

Profile 34 – P-40E-1 serial 41-36246, British serial ET892, squadron number 42, *Kay Strawberry Blonde / Pistoff Pat*

Lieutenant Sammy Pierce renamed this fighter *Kay Strawberry Blonde* when it was reassigned to him, while his crew chief added the name *Pistoff Pat* in cursive script on the starboard side. Pierce was flying this fighter when he claimed his first kill on 11 April 1943. When Pierce received a replacement P-40N he named it similarly. The original *Kay Strawberry Blonde*, which had many lives, is profiled as it appeared at Dobodura around March 1943.

Profile 35 – Curtiss P-40E serial 41-36171, squadron number 51, *Palm Beach Play Boy* (port cowl)/ *West Palm Beach* (starboard cowl)

First Lieutenant Clyde Barnett was assigned this P-40E refit in New Guinea in early 1943. Barnett named the fighter in honour of the enjoyable times he had spent at West Palm Beach in late 1941 when the 49th PG had been based at Morrison airfield. The circular painting on the rear fuselage was a beach landscape, with a small Donald Duck applied in front of the national insignia. Note also the large underwing stencil "US ARMY" has white piping applied.

PACIFIC PROFILES

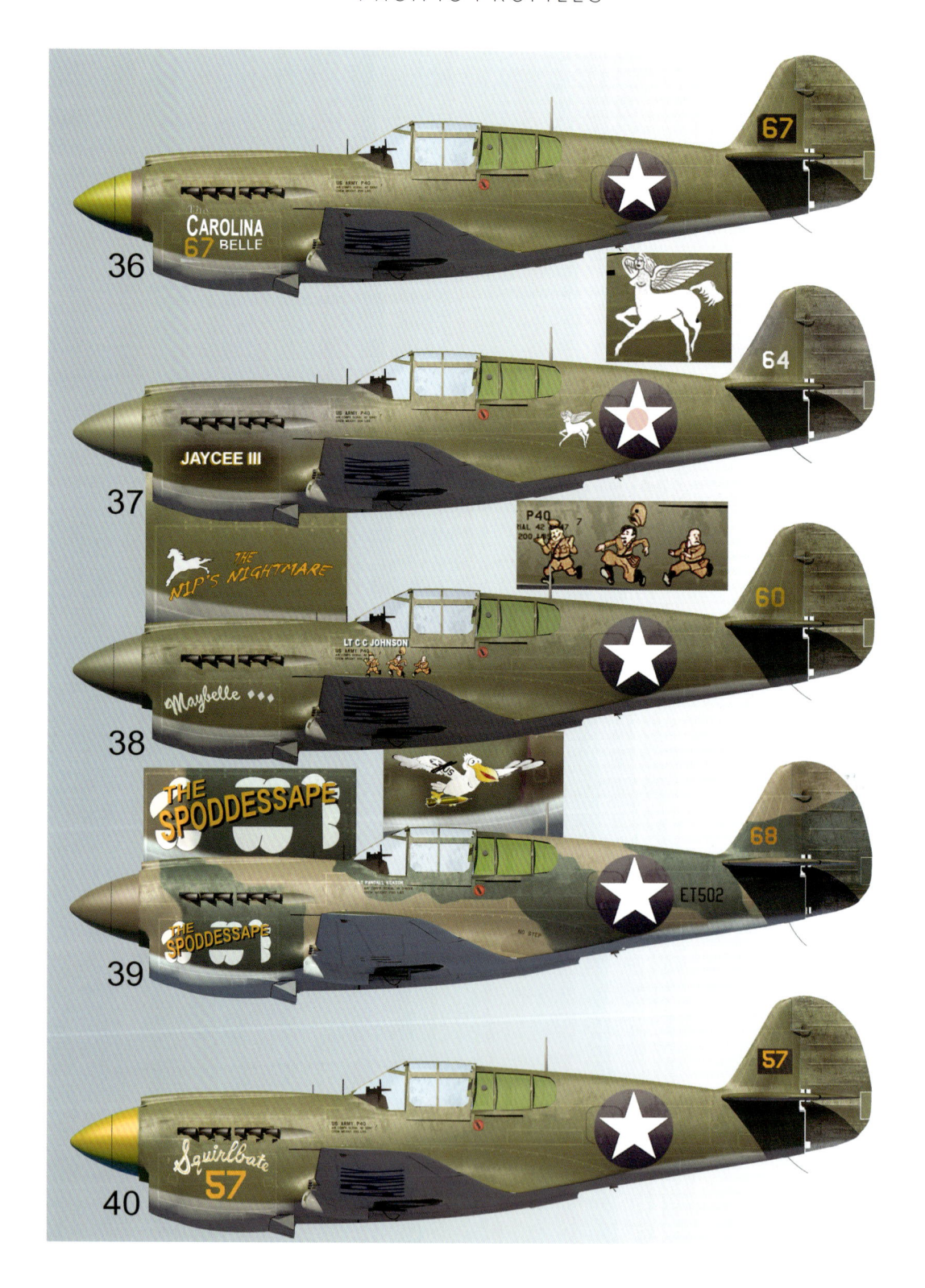

36

37

38

39

40

Profile 36 – P-40E serial 41-5611, squadron number 67, *Carolina Belle*

First Lieutenant Ernest Harris joined the 8th FS in New Guinea from Hawaii, earning him the nickname *Pineapple Man*. Note this has a smaller US fuselage insignia than the factory specification due to a field repair. It has been confused in previous publications with his later N model (see Profile 43), resulting in hybrid and incorrect profiles of his N model having a British camouflage scheme. Harris claimed his first kill in this P-40E on 7 January 1943, and flew it until receipt of his similarly named N model replacement.

Profile 37 – P-40E serial 40-681, (possible) squadron number 64, *Jaycee III*

After its previous life in Darwin as *Dollye* (see Prolife 28), this P-40E was sent to New Guinea with the 8th FS at the end of 1942 after it had been extensively rebuilt. In New Guinea the original red roundel started to show through from tropical weathering from where it had been overpainted around April 1942. The aircraft crashed at 17-Mile 'drome, Port Moresby, sometime in late 1942 or early 1943. Note it was assigned an 8th FS squadron number in the 60s, possibly 64, although this still needs confirmation (only the first digit "6" is visible in a photograph).

Profile 38 – P-40E serial 41-5481, squadron number 60, *The Nip's Nightmare / Maybelle*

This early E model Warhawk was ferried to Darwin where it was assigned to Lieutenant Charles Johnson. He first named the fighter *The Nip's Nightmare* as illustrated, with the running cartoon characters of Tojo, Hitler and Mussolini underneath the cockpit. He later renamed it *Maybelle* although it retained the character cartoons. As a result of a forced landing on 4 June 1942 in the Darwin area, the aircraft was transferred to a service squadron for repair. It was later converted into a two-seater (see Profile 104)

Profile 39 – P-40E-1 serial 41-25178, British serial ET502, squadron number 68, *Spoddessape*

This P-40E-1 was originally assigned in March 1942 to Captain Randall Keator at Darwin, who named it *Spoddessape*, a play on words for spotted-assed ape. The starboard cowl was decorated by the crew chief with artwork of a pelican with US insignia, toting shotguns strapped to its wings, and carrying a bomb. After the move to New Guinea, on 6 November 1942 Second Lieutenant Nelson Brownell was flying the aircraft when his engine suddenly seized over Kokoda and he crashed into jungle near Saga village. Brownell became the first fatality for the entire 49th FG in New Guinea.

Profile 40 – Curtiss P-40E 41-5314, squadron number 57, *Squirlbate*

This P-40E was assigned to and named by First Lieutenant Richard Vodra. In other publications it has been wrongly illustrated as Vodra's third assigned Warhawk, which was an N model with a chequered tail. Vodra had been a professional writer before the war and liked to play with words. His misspelling of "squirrel bait" was artistic and intentional. After claiming two fighters in May 1943, on 26 July 1943 Vodra nosed over *Squirlbate* in a muddy ditch at Dobodura and wrote it off.

PACIFIC PROFILES

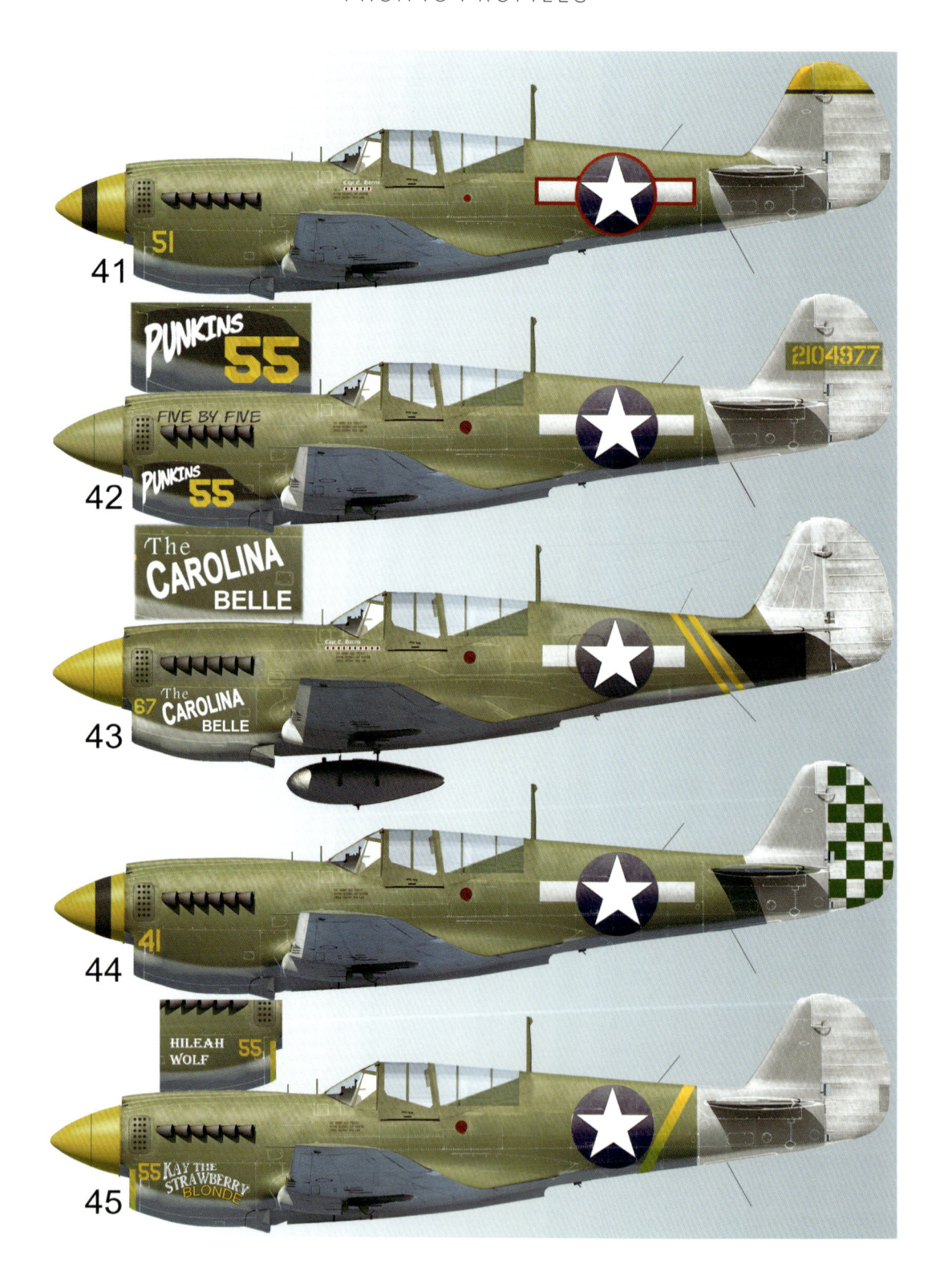

41

42

43

44

45

PAGE 52

Profile 41 – Curtiss P-40N-5 serial 42-105834, squadron number 51

First Lieutenant Donald Meuten went missing in this assigned Warhawk on 7 May 1944 shortly after the 8th FS had moved to Hollandia. Meuten was leading Red Flight when escorting B-24s on a mission against Biak. After turning back with engine problems, Meuten radioed that he was baling out but he was never found. The fighter retained the factory applied red-outline insignia until the day it was lost. It also carries the new 8th FS yellow-tip marking which had just started appearing.

Profile 42 – Curtiss P-40N-5 serial 42-104977, squadron number 55, *Punkins / Mr Five By Five*

First Lieutenant Joel Thorvaldson was assigned this N model at Horanda 'drome from another pilot in the second half of 1943. He renamed it *Punkins*, applied to the port cowl after his wife's nickname. The cowl was named *Mr Five By Five*, the crew chief's nickname for the fighter, just above the exhaust stack. Thorvaldson force-landed this P-40N on 13 September 1943 following a fight with JAAF Ki-61 and Ki-43-II fighters over Marilinen. After nine days in the jungle he was returned to his unit, while the isolated wreck was recovered in 2005 by helicopter. The components formed the basis to restore a P-40N to airworthy status in Australia in June 2009, before it was sold in the US where it still retains squadron number 55 to honour its wartime pedigree.

Profile 43 – Curtiss P-40N-5 serial 42-105947, squadron 67, *The Carolina Belle*

Named in honor of his home state, this fighter was the assigned mount of 8th FS commander Captain Ernest Harris and carried two yellow fuselage stripes to denote his leadership position. Harris had similarly named his first assigned Warhawk (see Profile 36). Just below the cockpit Harris painted a single row of Japanese flags to denote each of his aerial claims. Harris' most noteworthy mission in this P-40N unfolded on 7 January 1943 when he claimed three Ki-43 Oscars.

Profile 44 – Curtiss P-40N-5 serial 42-104986, squadron number 41

This N model was assigned to Captain Dan Moore and was the first in the 8th FS to acquire a chequered rudder. Moore applied the high-visibility rudder marking to underline a personal joke between himself and Lieutenant Joe Littleton, both from Louisiana. After Littleton was shot up by JAAF fighters over Wewak, Moore painted this rudder as a challenge to a mythical Japanese fighter the squadron had nicknamed *Wewak Willie*. Moore jibed Littleton that his extravagant rudder would entice "Wewak Willie" to come up and fight, so he could defend the honor of Louisiana. The practice was subsequently adopted by several other 7th and 8th FS pilots. Squadron number 41 was lost on 14 February 1944 after combat damage saw it force-land in the Ramu Valley.

Profile 45 – Curtiss P-40N-5 serial unknown, squadron number 55, *Kay the Strawberry Blonde / Haileah Wolf*

This fighter was in the first batch of N models allocated to the 8th FS and was assigned to First Lieutenant Samuel Pierce. Pierce's first assigned Warhawk was the similarly named P-40E-1 41-36246 (see Profile 34), which was lost in a crash outside Port Moresby on 12 December 1942. Pierce replicated the same name on this fighter when he received it at Dobodura in August 1943. The name *Haileah Wolf* was applied on the other side of the cowl by the crew chief who hailed from the town of Haileah in Florida. The fighter was lost to combat or an accident in late 1943.

PACIFIC PROFILES

Lieutenant William Day with his first Jerry, the predecessor to Jerry II as shown in Profile 33.

P-40E Dollye, as depicted in Profile 28, prior to its accident at Livingstone Field in June 1942.

P-40N squadron number 42 showcases one of the yellow and black spinner designs. Note that the underwing insignia lacks bars, indicating Kansas Kiddie III is an early P-40N-5.

Captain George Kiser with the lion motif on P-40E serial 41-5622, the subject of Profile 27.

The cartoons of Tojo, Hitler and Mussolini on P-40E The Nip's Nightmare, as depicted in Profile 38.

P-40E-1 41-35969 Scatterbrain, the subject of Profile 49, at Dobodura in early June 1943 just before it was lost. It still retains the original "bunyip" logo applied at Darwin.

First Lieutenant Robert McComsey at Darwin with the artwork of his wife on P-40E-1 serial 41-36089, as shown in Profile 47.

CHAPTER 5
9th Fighter Squadron "Flying Knights"

The 9th PS was one of three squadrons which comprised the 49th PG formed in the US in late 1941, as outlined in Chapter 3. It later adopted the name *Flying Knights* in Darwin. It arrived in Australia on 1 February 1942 under the leadership of Captain Victor Pixey. He was soon replaced by Jesse Peaselee and then during the defence of Darwin by Captain James Selman. In turn he was replaced by Captain Ben Irvin, when later on 30 July 1943 Selman was appointed the 49th FG commander.

When all three 49th PG squadrons were allocated experienced pilots who had survived the Philippines and Java campaigns, the 9th PS appointed Captain Ben Irvin, Lieutenant Joe Kruzel and Lieutenant Andy Reynolds as element leaders. The squadron was initially equipped with 25 Lend-Lease British P-40E-1s. On 8 March these left Williamtown in New South Wales to follow the inland route to Darwin. Two remained behind at Brisbane with engine trouble with two more stranded at Charleville for similar reasons. The remaining 21 proceeded to Cloncurry guided by a B-17E where two were written off because of heavy landings. The remaining nineteen then continued to Daly Waters on 14 March however four more force-landed when separated *en route* by heavy thunderstorms. The fifteen which actually made Daly Waters required three days to effect repairs. In the end from the original delivery flight which left Williamtown, only thirteen arrived at Darwin on 18 March, commencing patrols the next day. By the end of March 1942, the unit had regrouped to a strength of 21 P-40Es and 25 pilots.

Following several months of combat defending Darwin, the 9th FS left departed on 5 October 1942 and moved to Townsville. Unlike its sister units the 7th and 8th FS, its pilots were anticipating conversion to P-38s however considerable anguish ensued as a result. When the first Lightnings arrived in Townsville a few days later, an additional group of ex-Java veterans were assigned into the squadron and given preference for the P-38s. Many of the original 9th FS pilots waited for the rest of the month pending a decision on who was allocated what. Meanwhile the remainder ferried their Warhawks to Rorona (30-Mile) in New Guinea on 16 November, pending arrival of the P-38s. The first mission, escorting C-47s, unfolded the next day. The unit's last Warhawk mission was on 26 December 1942 from Three-Mile, Port Moresby.

Markings

The 9th FS applied squadron numbers in the 70 to 99 range, applied to the fin and sometimes to the forward cowl as well. Spinners were sometimes painted in the colour of the respective flight, i.e. Yellow, White or Red Flight.

The *Flying Knights* logo is a knight wearing head armour with bird wings attached. Its origins stem as far back as the March 1942 Darwin days when someone in 49th PG command quipped that the squadron's pilots reminded him of medieval knights who threw themselves into battle flailing around with no apparent cause.

PACIFIC PROFILES

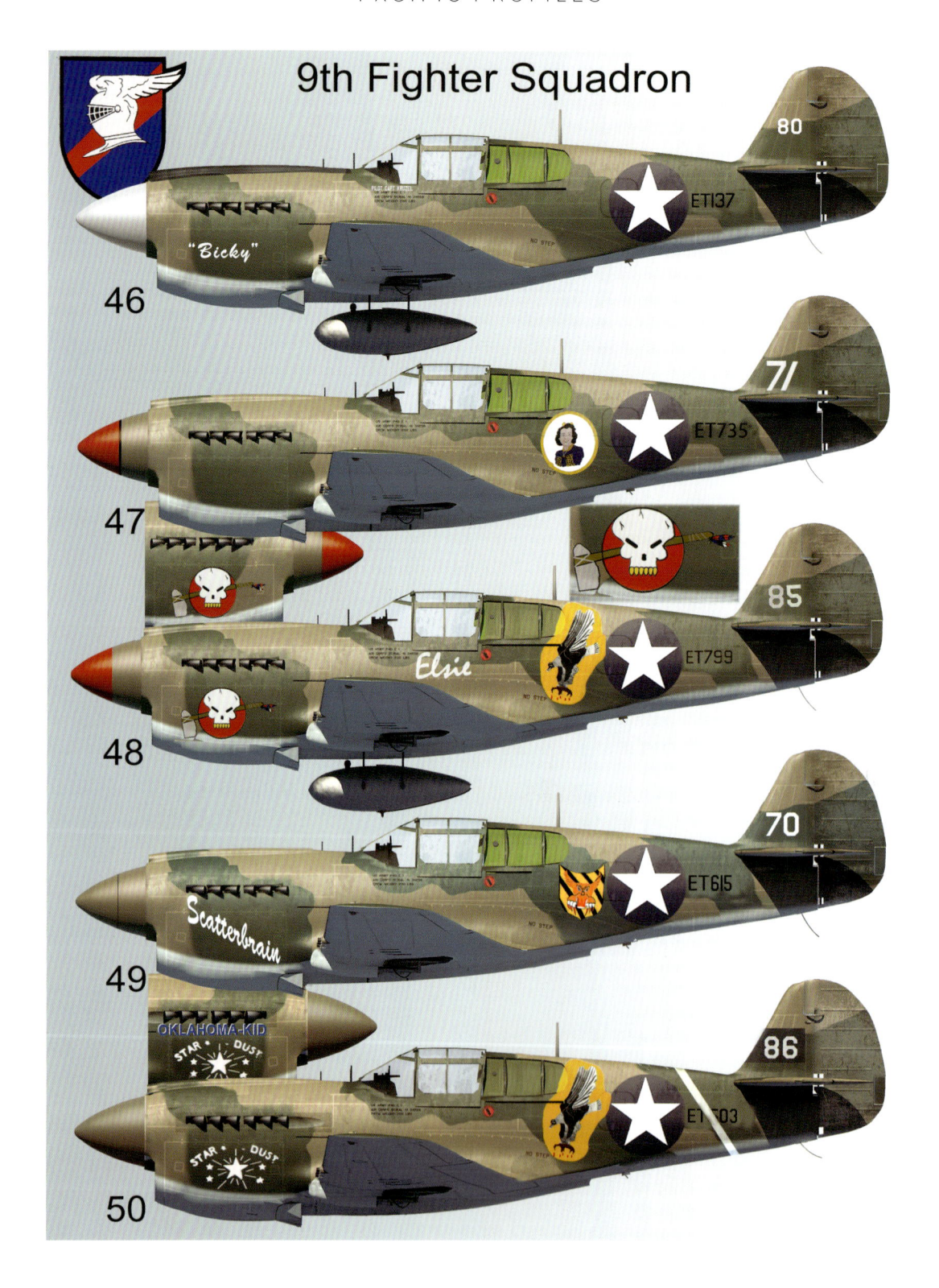

9th Fighter Squadron

46 — "Bicky" — 80 — ET137

47 — 71 — ET735

48 — Elsie — 85 — ET799

49 — Scatterbrain — 70 — ET615

50 — OKLAHOMA-KID / STAR·DUST — 86 — ET503

PAGE 58

Profile 46 – P-40E-1 serial 41-24813, British serial ET137, squadron number 80, *Bicky*

This Warhawk was allocated to the USAAF on 21 February 1942 and later assigned to First Lieutenant Joseph Kruzel who named the aircraft. It was wrecked on 3 August 1942 at Livingston airstrip during a taxi accident while being operated by the 49th FG maintenance officer Second Lieutenant Frederick Hollier. The airframe was then broken up for parts.

Profile 47 – P-40E-1 serial 41-36089, British serial ET735, squadron number 71

This Warhawk was assigned to First Lieutenant Robert McComsey at Darwin who decorated the rear fuselage with a painting of his wife. The aircraft was destroyed on 22 November 1942 in New Guinea when flown by Second Lieutenant Ralph Wire. That day it departed Three-Mile 'drome, Port Moresby, to escort C-47 transports bound for Dobodura Airfield. Wire abandoned his fighter due to an overheating engine and parachuted to earth near Myola.

Profile 48 – P-40E-1 serial 41-36153, British serial ET799, squadron number 85, *Elsie*

This Warhawk arrived in the 9th FS inventory in May 1942. It was assigned to First Lieutenant Clay Tice who delivered the aircraft to New Guinea in December after the move from Darwin. It carried the *Eagle Flight* logo also applied to fighters assigned to the B Flight quartet of Lieutenants Tice, Reynolds, Landers and Donalson. On 26 December 1942 Lieutenant Robert Vaught claimed two Japanese bombers when flying this aircraft. The fighter was then transferred to the 8th FS after the 9th FS converted to P-38s.

Profile 49 – P-40E-1 serial 41-35969, British serial ET615, squadron number 70, *Scatterbrain*

This P-40E-1 was assigned to First Lieutenant Clayton Peterson in Darwin as squadron number 77, and it was likely he who applied the "bunyip" insignia. At some stage thereafter it was renumbered as squadron number 70, with the name honouring the 1939 song *Scatterbrain*. The fighter moved to New Guinea where after a refit it was reassigned to Fifth Fighter Command Headquarters in early 1943. It was renamed *Dottie II* and given the new tail number 49 to reflect its 49th FG heritage. However, it was soon handed over to a service group where it crashed on 18 June 1943 while being used as a target towing aircraft.

Profile 50 – P-40E-1 serial 41-35957, British serial ET603, Squadron number 86, *Star Dust / Oklahoma Kid*

Star Dust was allocated squadron number 86 when it first entered service at Batchelor on 10 May 1942, assigned to Java veteran and flight leader First Lieutenant Andrew Reynolds. Named after a song popularised by Hollywood in 1940, Reynolds scored his final victory in *Star Dust* over Darwin on 30 July 1942. The aircraft is profiled as it appeared in early July 1942 just after the crew chief added *Oklahoma Kid* in blue with white shadow to the starboard cowl. The squadron number was applied over a matt black square, to enhance visibility, and the white forward-slanted flight leader marking was applied over the ET stencil. Confusion as to the precise identity of this fighter has arisen because all four of the 9th FS's *Eagle Flight* (B Flight) Warhawks sported the same diving eagle artwork.

PACIFIC PROFILES

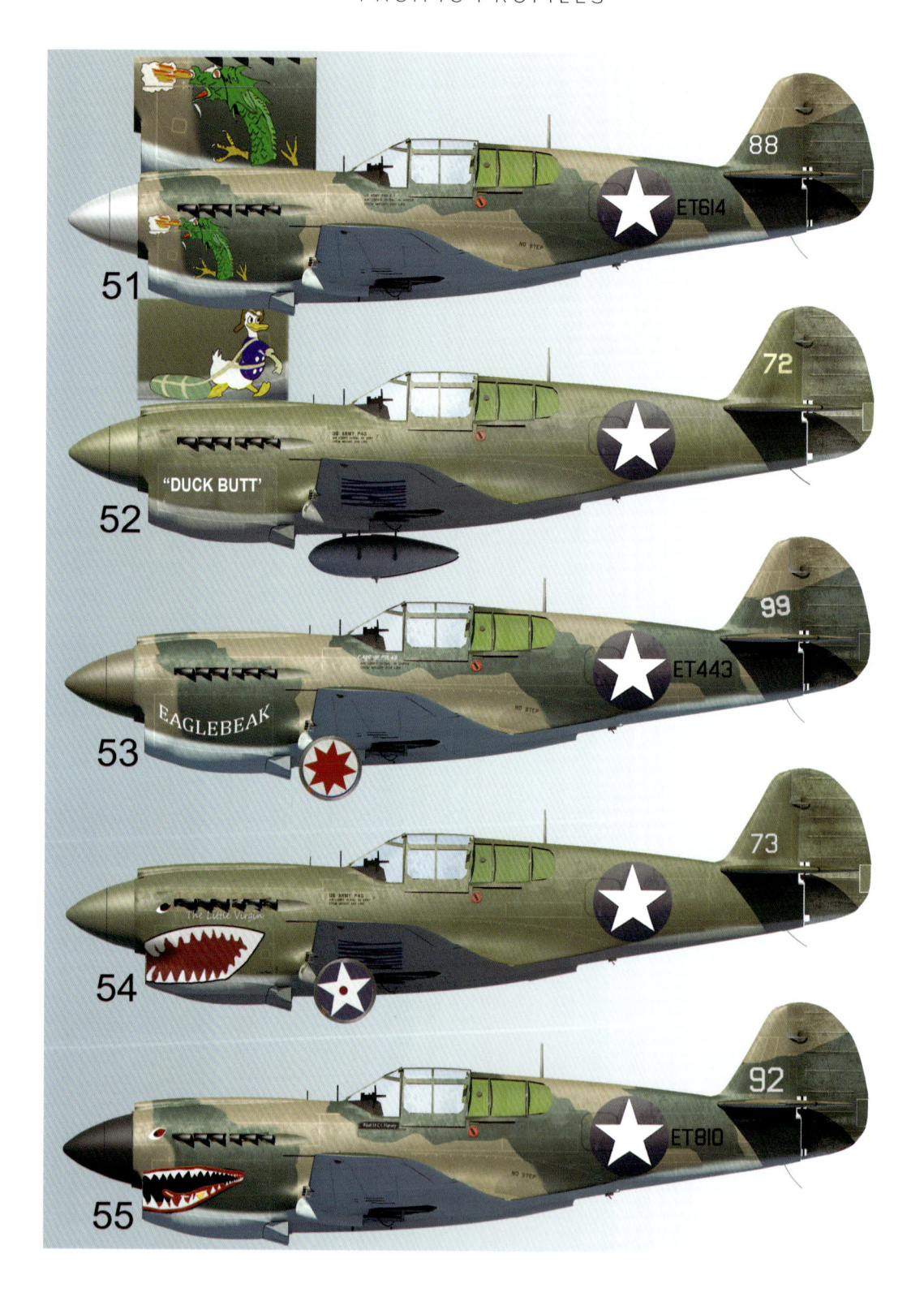

51

52 "DUCK BUTT"

53 EAGLEBEAK

54

55

Profile 51 – P-40E-1 serial 41-35968, British serial ET614, squadron number 88, (Dragon)

This model E-1 arrived at the 9th FS on 25 April 1942 and was assigned to *Dragon Flight*, in this case Second Lieutenant Deems Taylor. The dragon artwork appeared on both sides of the cowl and on all Warhawks in the flight, including First Lieutenant George Preddy's P-40E *Tarheel*. ET614 moved to New Guinea with the 9th FS, before being reassigned to a service squadron. It was finally removed from the Fifth Air Force inventory in May 1944.

Profile 52 – P-40E serial 41-5316, squadron number 72, *Duck Butt*

This Warhawk was in the first batch assembled at RAAF Amberley in January 1942. It arrived in the 9th FS inventory on 6 March 1942, allocated to First Lieutenant James Watkins, who named the aircraft after his nickname. This stemmed from the way he walked when carrying a parachute, and a waddling Donald Duck was painted on the starboard side of the cowl. The fighter was transferred to an RAAF service unit for refit on 7 October 1942, thence to No. 76 Squadron, RAAF, as A29-157. After an extended RAAF career, it ended its days on the Werribee bombing range west of Melbourne in 1948.

Profile 53 – P-40E-1 serial 41-25119, British serial ET443, Squadron number 99, *Eaglebeak*

This P-40E-1 was assigned to 9th FS commander Captain James Selman on 20 April 1942 after having been originally slated as A29-87 for the RAAF. Selman decorated the wheel hubs as illustrated and chose 99 as the last number in the 9th FS allocation of 70-99, a traditional number for squadron commanders. The number appeared at an angle but was straight when the fighter was parked. The fate of this Warhawk is unknown save that it was not lost to combat.

Profile 54 – P-40E 40-677, squadron number 73, *The Little Virgin*

This early P-40E was assigned to wiry Java veteran First Lieutenant Bill Levitan and assigned squadron number 73. Levitan named it *The Little Virgin* and decorated the cowl with a distinctive shark-mouth. Levitan was highly regarded as a teacher of combat techniques to the incoming junior 49th FG fighter pilots. The wheel hubs were decorated with a US insignia. Levitan himself went missing in action on 3 March 1943, while ferrying a P-38 from Townsville to Port Moresby.

Profile 55 – P-40E-1 serial 41-36164, British serial ET810, squadron number 92

This Warhawk was the third of four in the 9th FS to receive a cowl shark-mouth, and the second among these to include a tongue. The fighter was Second Lieutenant Clyde Harvey's third number 92 after he experienced two previous misadventures. The resultant subsequent airframe transfers underline the challenges of unwrapping the markings of all 49th FG squadrons. On 8 May 1942, when flying his first 92 (P-40E 41-5614), Harvey landed on the main Darwin road mistaking it for Livingstone strip. As a result, one wing collided with a water pipe, however repairs were quickly made. Then, three days later when flying his second 92 (P-40E-1 ET491), Harvey force-landed at Middle Point near Darwin when his engine failed. Harvey was then issued this third 92 which he bellied in at Livingston Field on 4 September 1942. The airframe was repaired and returned to service with the 8th FS.

PACIFIC PROFILES

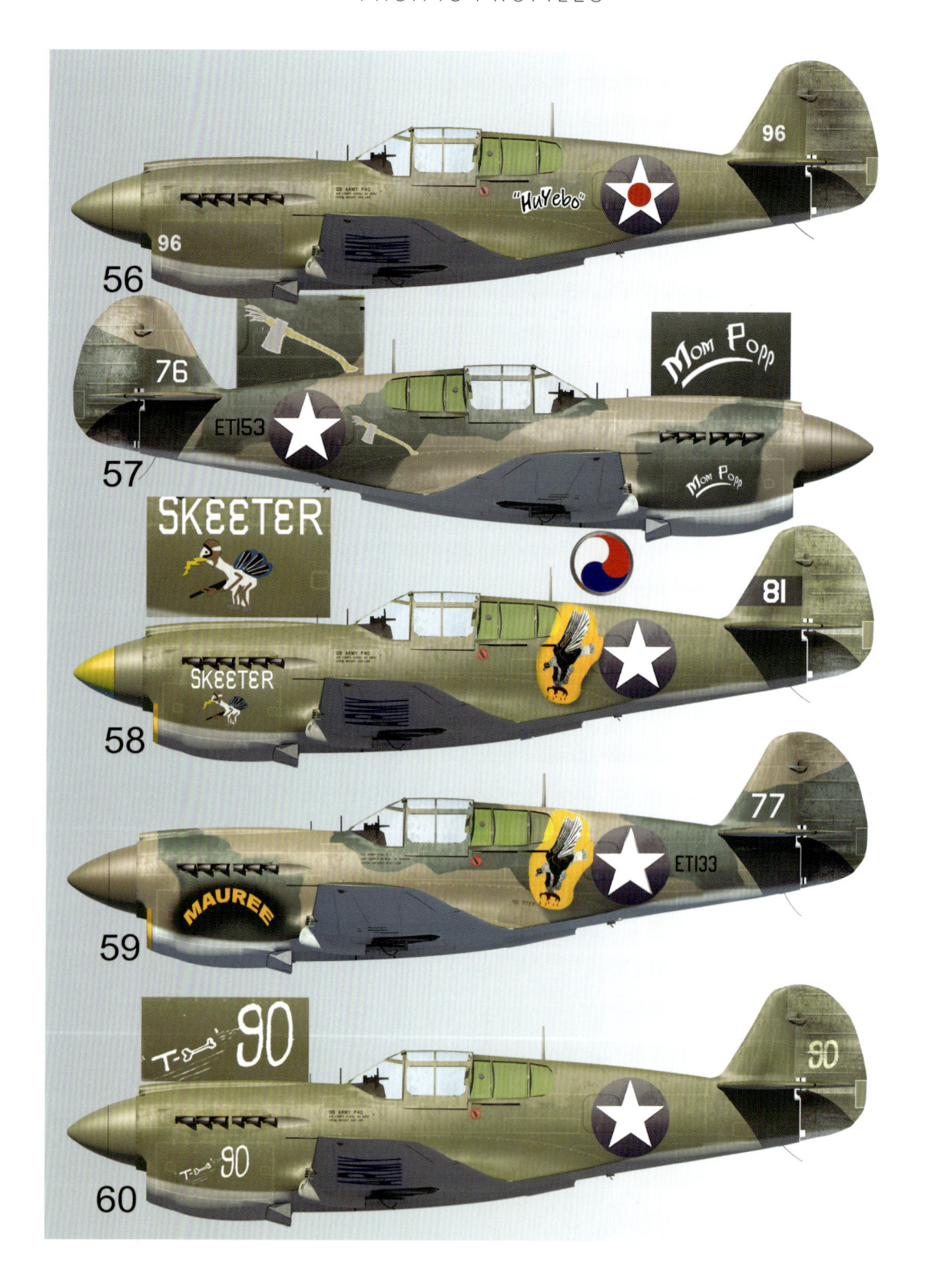

Profile 56 – P-40E serial 41-5638, squadron number 93, *Huyebo*

This fighter was assigned to Second Lieutenant Stephan "Polly" Poleschuk of Belarus-American heritage. He named it *Huyebo*, a slang word in his local dialect which translates as "not worth much". This was a humorous reference to a comment by 49th FG commander Major Paul Wurtsmith who had once told him that his landing skills were just that. This fighter is unique as it is credited on 22 March 1942 with the squadron's first aerial victory, a No. 3 *Ku* C5M2 Babs flying a reconnaissance mission over Darwin. The Babs crew was unlucky to have been separated from its escort of three Zeros, and it was found by a quartet of Warhawks. After they returned to base, Poleschuk and Second Lieutenant Clyde Harvey tossed a coin for the victory, and it was awarded to Poleschuk. The fighter is profiled as it appeared on the day of the interception. It was written off three months later on 16 June 1942.

Profile 57 – P-40E serial 41-24829, British serial ET153, squadron number 76, *Mom Popp*

This British Warhawk was assembled in Australia in February 1942 and was first assigned as number 5 in the 49th PG's Headquarters Flight on 1 March 1942 at Bankstown. It was later issued to Second Lieutenant Floyd Finberg as number 93 until 25 August 1942 when there was a shuffle of pilots between the 9th FS's various flights, resulting in the fighter being renumbered as 76. It is unknown who painted the name *Mom Popp* on the starboard cowl.

Profile 58 – P-40E serial 41-5647, squadron number 81, *Skeeter*

Assembled on 6 March 1942, this fighter became First Lieutenant John Lander's *Skeeter* of *Eagle Flight* prior to it becoming the RAAF's A29-159 on 7 September 1942. It was one of the last seven delivered to the RAAF during September 1942 from USAAF Stocks. On 19 February 1943 it was transferred to No. 75 Squadron, RAAF, following repairs and given the squadron code "C". The RAAF pilots liked *Skeeter*'s artwork sufficiently that they retained it on the cowl. After considerable RAAF use, in 1948 it was destroyed as a target on the Werribee bombing range.

Profile 59 – P-40E-1 serial 41-24809, British serial ET133, Squadron number 77, *Mauree*

This Warhawk was Second Lieutenant Jack Donalson's (not Donaldson) first assigned fighter with the same name, and part of *Eagle Flight*. It was wrecked on 16 July 1942 when Donalson collided with a tree and while landing south of Livingstone airstrip, with Donalson receiving only minor injuries. Donalson's second P-40 was ET736 which was destroyed during another landing accident at Darwin on 26 August 1942, this time flown by First Lieutenant John Landers.

Profile 60 – P-40E serial unknown, squadron number 90, *T-(bone)*

Little is known of this P-40E save it was assigned in early 1942 to the 9th FS in Darwin and was likely in the 41-5XXX range. Its name is a rarity of combined alphabet and artwork.

PACIFIC PROFILES

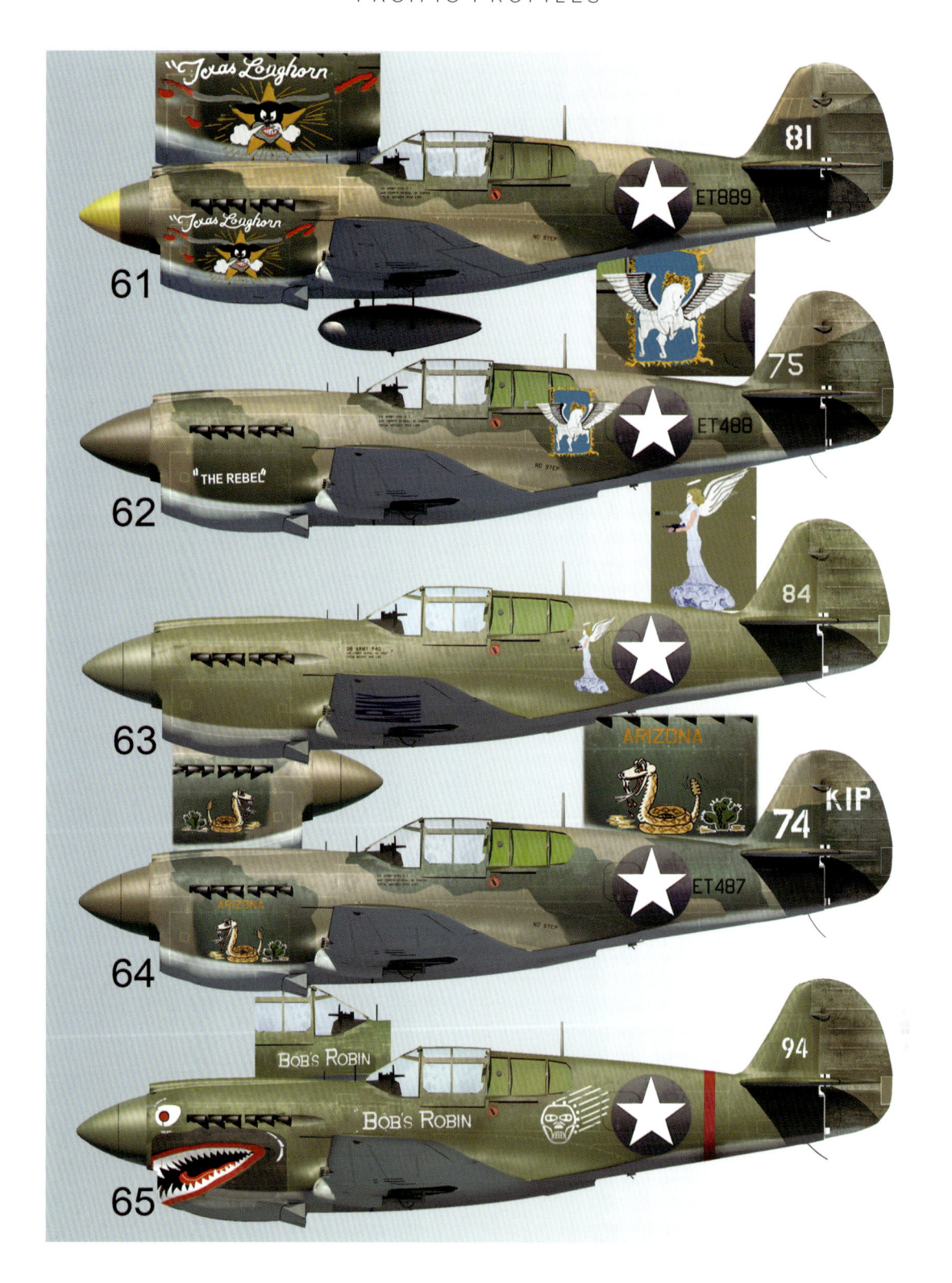

61

62

63

64

65

PAGE 64

Profile 61 – P-40E-1 serial 41-36243, British serial ET889, squadron number 81, *Texas Longhorn*

The identity of this Warhawk has been confused over the years as a result of misinterpretation of the ET number. It is sometimes wrongly illustrated elsewhere as ET603. ET899 was issued to the USAAF on 4 June 1942 and then ferried to Batchelor strip. It replaced First Lieutenant Andrew Reynolds' previous Warhawk *Star Dust* (see Profile 50). When the 9th FS moved to Townsville to convert to the Lockheed Lightning, this Warhawk was among those transferred to the 8th FS in New Guinea, retaining the *Texas Longhorn* art. It was lost on 1 March 1943 when flown by Lieutenant Cyrus Lynd, near Kokoda. The Warhawk is portrayed as it appeared on the day of its loss with the 8th FS.

Profile 62 – P-40E-1 41-25164, British serial ET488, squadron number 75, *The Rebel*

Assigned to the squadron at Darwin on 9 March 1942, this British E-1 Warhawk sported a unique winged Pegasus motif on the rear fuselage. Assigned to Captain Ben Irvin, the fighter was lost in combat when flown by First Lieutenant John Landers over Pongani in New Guinea on 26 December 1942. That day Landers led White Flight on a patrol over Dobodura when they clashed with 11th *Sentai* Ki-43-I Oscar fighters. Landers baled out a low altitude and was returned to his unit after spending five days in the jungle.

Profile 63 – P-40E unknown serial, squadron number 84, (angel motif)

Second Lieutenant James Angel was likely posted to the 9th FS in May 1942 and was allocated this P-40E. Angel blew out a tyre on 20 May 1942 at Adelaide River however he returned to make a safe landing. The serial number of this fighter continues to elude historians, and elsewhere it has incorrectly been illustrated as a camouflaged P-40E-1.

Profile 64 – P-40E-1 serial 41-25163, British serial ET487, squadron number 74, *Arizona / KIP*

This Warhawk was assigned to and named by Lieutenant Sid Woods at Darwin and was also often flown by Second Lieutenant Russell Francis. Woods, who grew up in Yuma, Arizona, was later promoted to major and appointed as the 9th FS Operations Officer. The aircraft went to New Guinea in late 1942 where it was written off during an operational accident at 17-Mile 'drome on 1 December 1942. The name *KIP* appeared in capitals on the rudder, the name of a girl Woods knew back in the US. The rattlesnake art appeared on both sides of the cowl in slightly different versions. This aircraft was retrieved post-war and is currently restored in the US today.

Profile 65 – P-40E-1 serial 41-24872, British serial ET196, squadron number 94, *Bob's Robin*

After early service with the 7th FS, this P-40E-1 was reassigned to the 9th FS in April 1942. Oddly, as a British Warhawk, it is listed as having an ex-factory Olive Drab paint scheme. First Lieutenant Robert Vaught named and decorated the fighter and was flying it on 16 July 1942 when he was bitten by a poisonous snake which had hidden in the cockpit. He put down to seek help, but not finding any, flew back to base the following day. The aircraft was finally written off following an accident on 6 September 1942. It was one of the four shark-mouth airframes in the 9th FS and the red vertical stripe indicated Vaught's status as a flight leader.

PACIFIC PROFILES

Captain Ben Irvin with the Pegasus motif on P-40E-1 41-25164 The Rebel, as shown in Profile 62.

P-40E-1 41-25119 Eaglebeak, as depicted in Profile 53, has its guns tested during the Darwin campaign.

First Lieutenant John Angel with his appropriately adorned P-40E, as illustrated in Profile 63.

P-40E-1 41-35957 Star Dust in flight with P-40E-1 41-35969 Scatterbrain during the Darwin air campaign. These are depicted in Profiles 50 and 49 respectively.

P-40E T-(bone), as illustrated in Profile 60, under camouflage netting at Darwin.

First Lieutenant Robert Vaught atop P40E-1 Bob's Robin, the subject of Profile 65. One of the wrecked hangars at RAAF Darwin is visible in the background.

P-40N-5 42-105521 Miss Innocence, as shown in Profile 73, at the northern side of Three-Mile 'drome, Port Moresby.

A new 35th FS P-40N arrives at Three-Mile 'drome, Port Moresby. The wartime censor has obscured the serial number. Note the black piping on the leading edge of the white wing.

CHAPTER 6
35th Fighter Squadron "Black Panthers"

The 8th FG comprised the 35th, 36th and 80th FS and on 26 April 1942 fifteen 35th FS Airacobras moved to New Guinea as the first forward deployed USAAF fighter squadron to face the Japanese in the theatre. Following months of fighting from Port Moresby airfields, then after leave in Australia, the 35th FS returned to New Guinea, followed by a rest period at Mareeba in north Queensland in late February until May 1943 where they continued using Airacobras for training. After recall to Port Moresby the squadron equipped with P-40N-5 Warhawks at Kila 'drome in October 1943, whilst the 36th and 80th FS transitioned to P-47s and P-38s respectively. There was considerable resentment by the other two squadrons against the 80th FS for acquiring the favoured Lockheed Lighting ahead of them. During its time in New Guinea the 35th FS used the callsign "Brandy".

The main 35th FS commander during the P-40N era was Major Emmett "Cyclone" Davis who oversaw the conversion from Airacobras to Warhawks. He was replaced by Major Harold McClelland in January 1944. The squadron's Warhawk inventory consisted exclusively of late N-5 models in the serial range 42-105107 to 42-105745. The one exception was M model serial 43-5521, assigned to First Lieutenant Harold Souther. The N models were first received at Kila 'drome before the squadron took them to Finschhafen on 25 December 1943. It moved to Cape Gloucester on 19 February 1944, then to Nadzab on 14 March 1944 where it took delivery of its first Lightnings at the end of the month. The squadron left the main New Guinea theatre in July 1944, taking its new P-38s to Owi Island on the first of that month.

Markings

Following on from the 35th FS's Airacobra era, each Warhawk was assigned an individual alphabetical letter, painted on both sides of the cowl panel in yellow. The forward half of each spinner was painted yellow. All tailplanes and wing leading edges were painted white in accordance with orders to identify Allied fighters, however unique to the 35th FS, most leading edge white wings and tailplane demarcations were bordered with black piping. The 35th FS logo was a running black panther with a red tongue against a silver background.

P-40N-5 "P" parked on the northern side of Three-Mile 'drome, Port Moresby, with Mount Baldy in the background. Most aircraft also carried a black border on the white tailplane marking.

35th Fighter Squadron

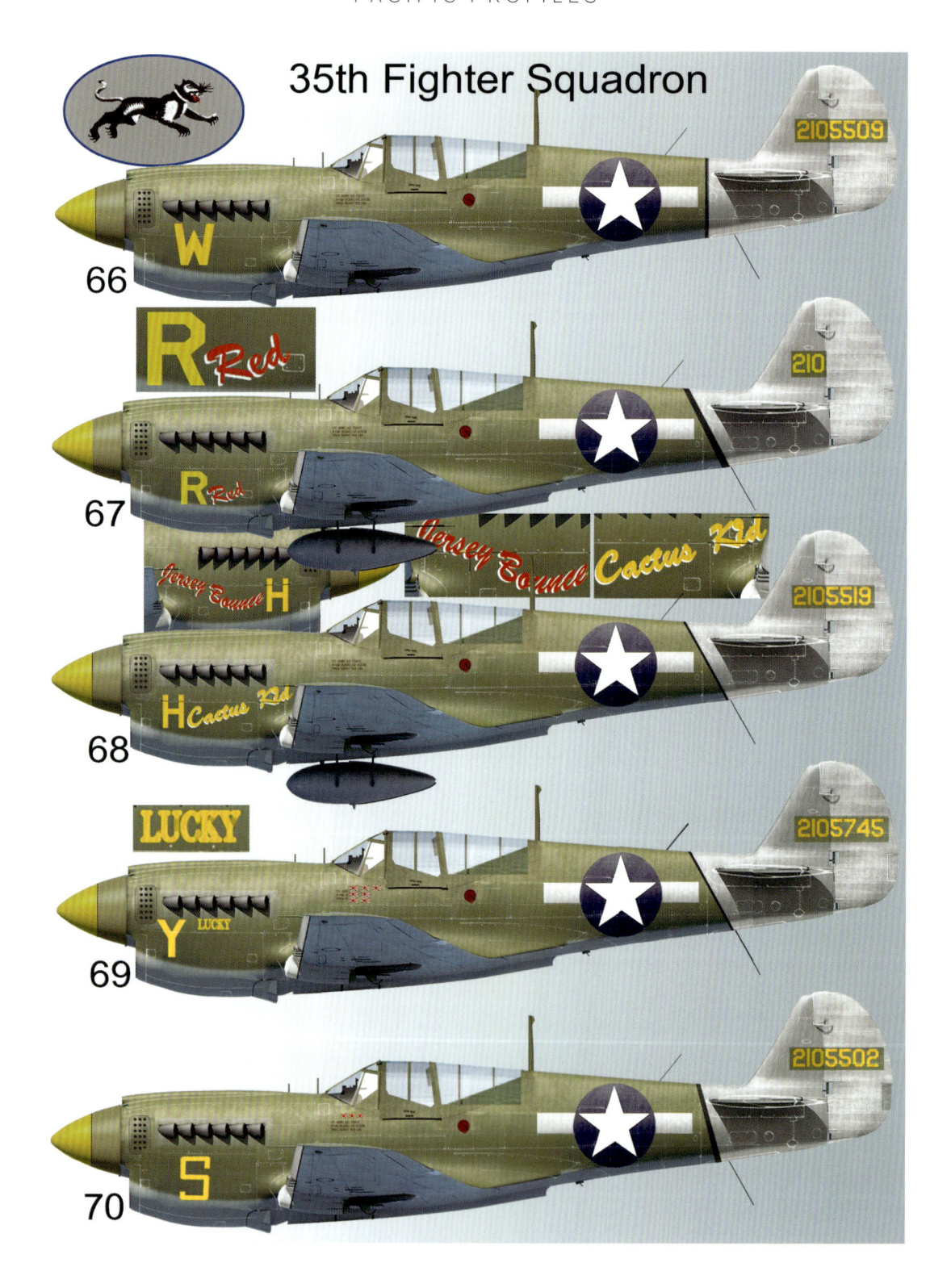

Profile 66 – P-40N-5 serial 42-105509, squadron letter W

On 15 November 1943 eight 35th FS P-40Ns departed Nadzab to patrol from Kaiapit to Lae. Over Kaiapit, the formation encountered Japanese Ki-43-II Oscar fighters from the 248th and 59th *Sentai*. During the ensuing combat, Lieutenant Richard West attacked a Japanese fighter which was chasing Lieutenant Robert Parker before Parker in turn made a diving turn and engaged a fighter on West's tail. Parker then collided with one of the Oscars tearing off the starboard wings of both fighters and causing Parker's P-40N to spin into jungle north of Kaiapit. West followed the spinning P-40N (illustrated here) down low but did not observe the crash due to low cloud. Later that afternoon two 35th FS pilots returned to the Kaiapit area to search for Parker's P-40N but failed to locate it. In May 2019 Parker's remains were collected from the crash site 76 years after he was lost.

Profile 67 – P-40N-5 serial unknown, squadron letter R, *Red*

Named by First Lieutenant "Red" Stonacker, this Warhawk was also flown regularly by Lieutenant Thomas Alsop.

Profile 68 – P-40N-5 serial 42-105519, squadron letter H, *Cactus Kid / Jersey Bounce*

This Warhawk was written off when First Lieutenant Harold Souther had a landing accident at Finschhafen airstrip. Placed under the care of crew chief Sergeant Ray Shelton, the fighter was replaced by the squadron's only M model, serial 43-5521.

Profile 69 – P-40N-5 serial 42-105745, squadron letter Y, *Lucky*

Lucky was named and assigned to First Lieutenant Richard "Dick" West, who had the name applied after he claimed four aerial victories over Kaiapit on 15 November 1943 against Ki-43-II Oscars and Ki-21 Sally bombers. The name was applied on both sides of the cowls.

Profile 70 – P-40N-5 serial 42-105502, squadron letter S

First Lieutenant Roy Klandrud applied three victory markings to this P-40N-5 following aerial claims he made on 22 September, 26 November and 26 December 1943 when flying this fighter. Klandrud later converted to P-38s and returned to the US in October 1944.

A line-up of 35th FS Warhawks at Cape Gloucester in February 1944, with a visiting Beechcraft C-45 in the background.

PACIFIC PROFILES

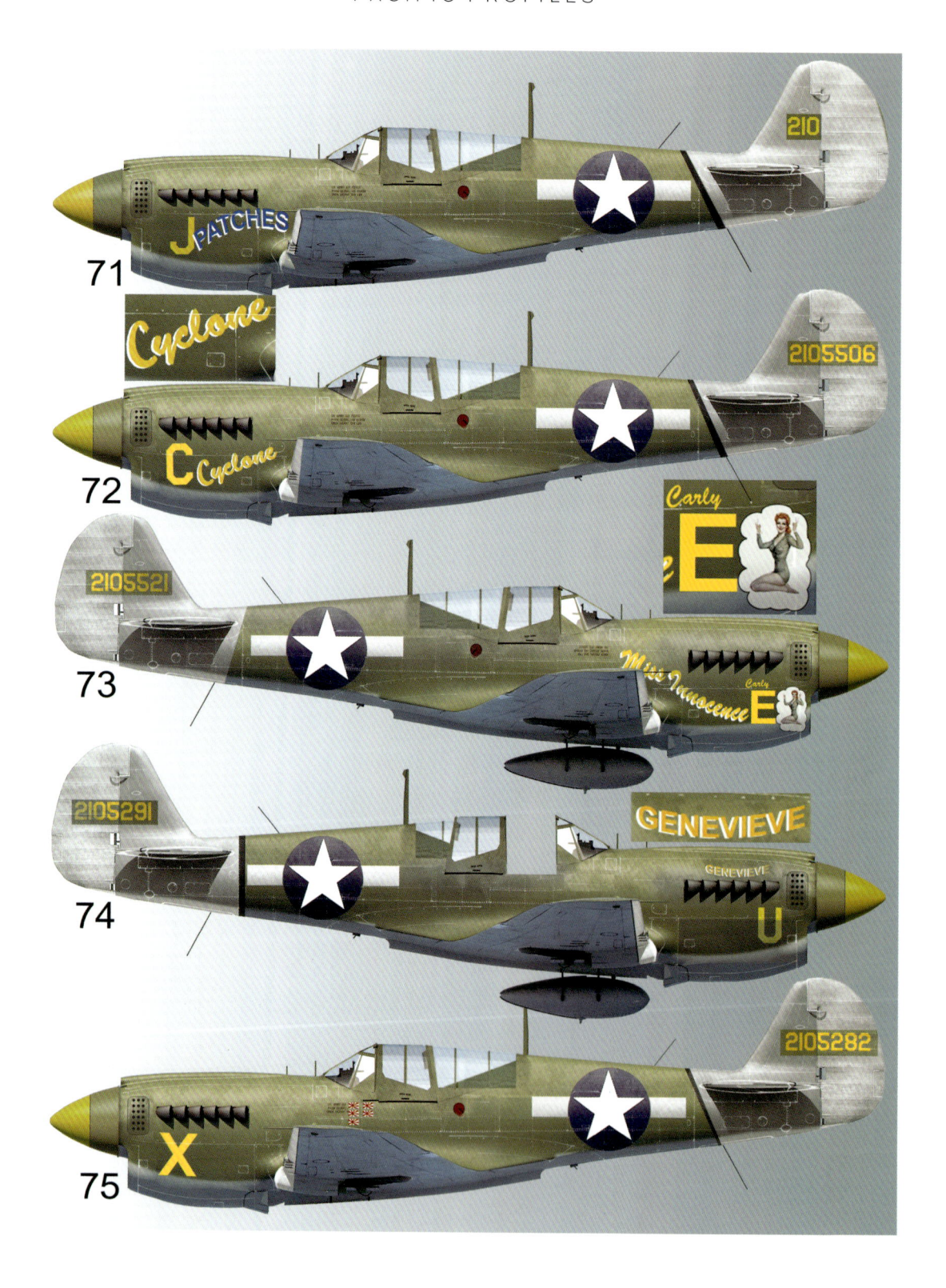

Profile 71 – P-40N-5 serial unknown, squadron letter J, *Patches*

This fighter received a replacement rudder at Cape Gloucester; thus its full serial number is unknown.

Profile 72 – P-40N-5 serial 42-105506, squadron letter C, *Cyclone*

This fighter was assigned to the 35th FS commander Major Emmett "Cyclone" Davis, who acquired the nickname from his time in Hawaii due to his adept aircraft handling skills. Davis oversaw the squadron's conversion from Airacobras to Warhawks and claimed six aerial victories when flying this mount with his first on 27 September 1943. He later became commander for the parent 8th FG during the subsequent P-38 era.

Profile 73 – P-40N-5 serial 42-105521, squadron letter E, *Miss Innocence*

The fighter was one of the few in the 35th FS to have Vargas nose-art applied.

Profile 74 – P-40N-5 serial 42-105291, squadron letter U, *Genevieve*

Lieutenant Fred Boerman named this P-40N-5 *Genevieve*, and the airframe was maintained by crew chief Sergeant Jerry Nolan.

Profile 75 – P-40N-5 serial 42-105282, squadron letter X

Lieutenant James Brewer was assigned this fighter at Cape Gloucester.

P-40N-5 serial 42-105502 "S", as illustrated in Profile 70, parked on the southern side of Nadzab #1 where Lake Wanum is hidden in the hills behind right. This aircraft is often misidentified as a 7th FS Warhawk, confusing the S as the numeral 5.

P-40F Destitute Prostitute, as shown in Profile 79, at Munda on 14 August 1943. It was one of the first Allied aircraft to land on the captured airfield.

Lieutenant Cotesworth Head poses with brand-new P-40M 43-5673. It will soon be assigned to First Lieutenant Frank Gaunt who named it The Twerp (see Profile 83).

CHAPTER 7
44th Fighter Squadron "Vampires"

Assigned to the 18th PG, the 44th PS was activated at Wheeler Field, Hawaii, on 22 November 1940. It was redesignated as the 44th FS on 15 May 1942. It became the first of only two Thirteenth Air Force Squadrons to use the P-40. An advanced echelon arrived at Bauerfield, Efate, in the New Hebrides in November 1942 commanded by Major Kermit Tyler. Here it first operated short-fuselage P-40F-1s, starting combat with the type from Guadalcanal in December 1942. The first five Warhawks assigned into the inventory were flown off the USS *Nassau* on 11 November 1942 to Pelikulo Airfield on Espiritu Santo, where they were test-flown and later ferried down to Bauerfield. The squadron was tasked with the air defence of the New Hebrides, enabling a dozen F4F-4 Wildcats held in reserve there to be forwarded to Guadalcanal.

The first 44th FS losses were non-combat related when on 20 December 1942 a flight of P-40Fs became lost during a training exercise and force-landed on the island of Erromango (see Profile 76). The unit commenced combat operations from Fighter #1 on Guadalcanal in January 1943, before moving a few months later to Fighter #2. Major John Little replaced Tyler as squadron commander on 24 May 1943, and on 14 August 1943 a detachment forward deployed to Munda shortly after its capture, constituting the first Allied aircraft to use the field.

By mid-1943 moves were afoot to convert the unit to the Lockheed Lightning and Major Robert Westbrook was appointed as the new squadron commander on 25 September 1943 to oversee the transition. Although the USAAF did not classify the 44th FS as a twin-engine fighter unit until 20 February 1944, several Warhawk pilots were seconded to other Lightning units as early as September 1943 in preparation for the transition. In January 1944 the squadron said goodbye to its last Warhawk when it relocated back to Guadalcanal to receive its first batch of P-38Hs followed by early model Olive Drab P-38Js. Its last Warhawk combat losses were three downed on 8 November 1943 during a mission to Torokina. It lost a total of fourteen Warhawks in the South Pacific theatre: one accidentally shot down by a F4F Wildcat on 4 February 1943, seven to combat and six more to other causes.

Markings

The 44th FS's first batch of short-fuselage P-40F-1s sent to the New Hebrides comprised just five new airframes in the serial range 41-14101 to 41-14106. Unusually, at least for a USAAF squadron, it allocated commensurate squadron numbers which aligned with the last three digits of each airframe, illustrated in Profiles 77, 78 and 81. Another batch of five was delivered in mid-December from Hawaii, which had the original 18th PG rear fuselage band, as described below, later complemented by the first batch of long-fuselage P-40F-15s in the serial range 41-19819 to 41-19844. The first of these arrived at Efate in January 1943, after which it received its first P-40Ms in June 1943 in the serial range 43-5489 to 43-5813.

The 44th FS numbered its Warhawks in the 101 to 150 range, in the one-hundred series, whereas

Warhawks from the 68th FS were numbered in the two-hundred series. Both squadrons used the F model which had a Rolls-Royce V-1650 Merlin engine installed instead of an Allison V-1710 which powered the P-40E series. The Rolls-Royce gave improved high-altitude performance and understandably was liked by its pilots.

A single white vertical band was already applied to 44th FS Warhawks which had seen original service in Hawaii. This was an 18th PG marking and a later second forward stripe extended on the top and under surface of the wing. The rationale of the second stripe was to facilitate identification of the type as Allied, following several occasions on which Warhawks had been fired at by "friendlies". Sometimes an oblique white band extended across the fin. By late June 1943 most tailplanes had been painted all white to further assist the process, with a variety of applications sometimes masking the serial number. The shark-mouth marking was unique to the squadron's sister unit, the 68th FS, however airframe swaps between the two were commonplace, resulting in the appearance of several shark-mouths in the 44th FS inventory (Profiles 78 & 85 being examples). Around 40 Warhawks served in the unit before it transitioned to the Lockheed Lightning.

The original logo was designed by Walt Disney and featured a critter firing a machine-gun whilst held in a stork's beak. Although this logo appears nowhere in official histories, it was used during the early Guadalcanal campaign and appeared outside unit offices. It was later replaced by a logo of a vampire face bearing blooded teeth sometime in the first half of 1944. This logo is more closely associated with the unit in WWII.

P-40F-15 41-19825 Miss Alma, the subject of Profile 82, in formation with a short-fuselage 68th FS Warhawk over Solomons skies.

P-40M squadron number 137 at Munda following an accident around August 1943.

P-40M 43-5684 Princess Pat II, as illustrated in Profile 87, refuels at Munda on 14 August 1943.

The starboard side of P-40F Reckless Prostitute, as shown in Profile 79 at Munda in September 1943. Crew chief Staff Sergeant James Cooley has painted fourteen Japanese flags under the canopy, representing the cumulative score from all the Warhawks he had maintained.

P-40F-1 41-14105 was among the first batch of Warhawks flown off the USS Nassau on 11 November 1942 to Espiritu Santo. The squadron number 105 showcases the early style of stenciling. The name Betty was applied by its crew chief.

44TH FIGHTER SQUADRON "VAMPIRES"

First Lieutenant Frank Gaunt flying P-40M serial 43-5673 The Twerp, as shown in Profile 83, over the north coast of Guadalcanal

P-40F-15 41-19827 Phoebe, the subject of Profile 85, at Fighter Two on Guadalcanal in January 1943.

P-40F-15 116 (as shown in Profile 89) in front of P-40F-15 111 Destitute Prostitute (Profile 79) at Guadalcanal's Fighter Two in late 1943.

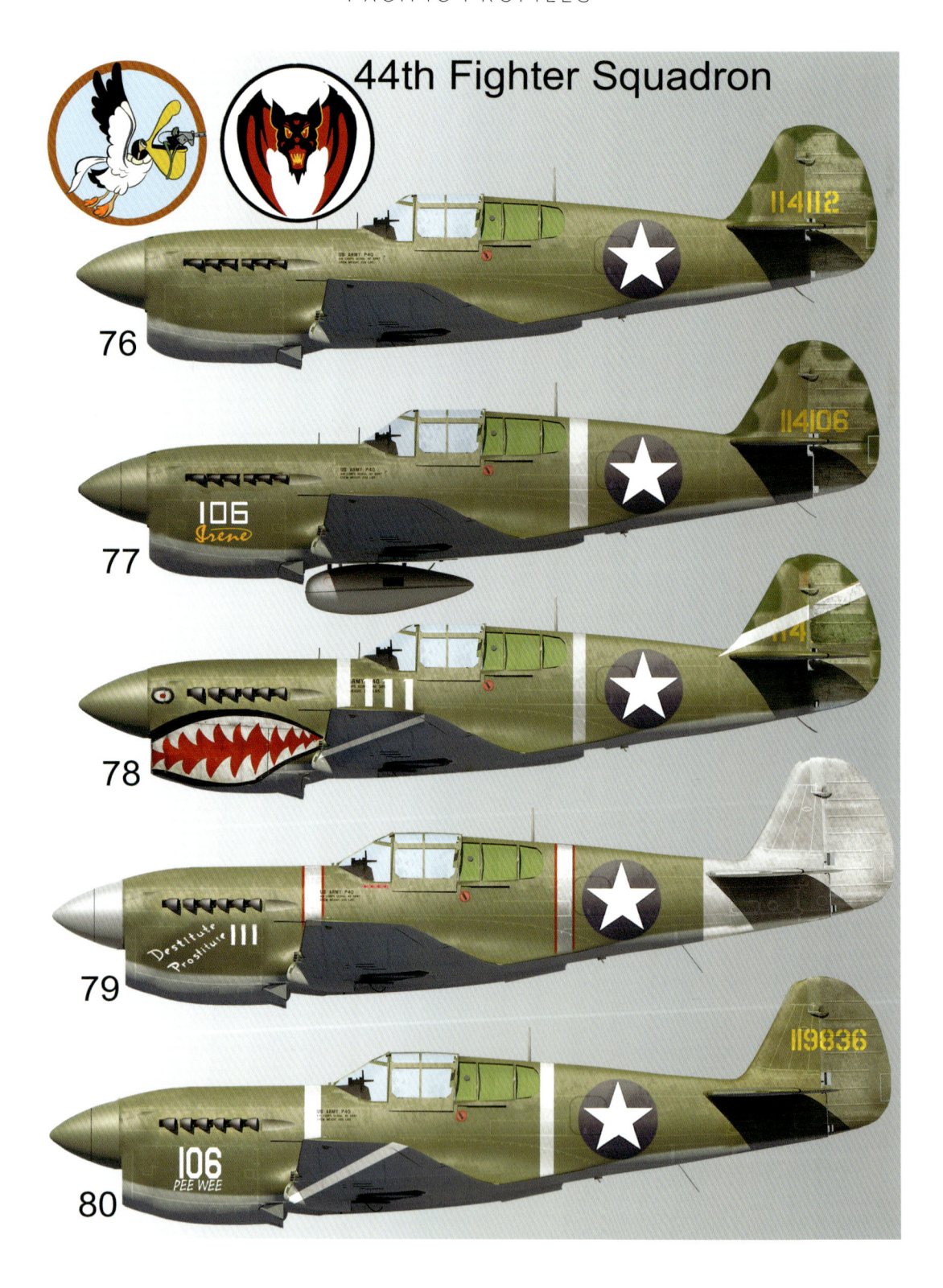

44th Fighter Squadron

Profile 76 – P-40F-1 serial 41-14112

This early P-40F model was among the second batch of fighters assigned into the 44th FS at Bauerfield, when it was still waiting allocation of a squadron number. The new fighter flew several uneventful training routines around New Hebrides airspace until 20 December 1942 when it was one of four Warhawks which departed Bauerfield for a navigation exercise. The return leg went awry when bad weather blocked the way home ensuring all four force-landed on the island of Erromango, 80 miles to the south-southeast of Bauerfield. The four force-landed in a clearing atop an elevated plain, with all pilots uninjured. This fighter, profiled the day it force-landed, was salvaged after the war and restored to flying status in Australia, with its first reborn flight occurring on 22 April 2009.

Profile 77 – P-40F-1 serial 41-14106, squadron number 106, *Irene*

This early P-40F model was among the first batch of fighters assigned into the 44th FS at Bauerfield. It was allocated squadron number 106, applied using masking tape. It was delivered with an extant single rear white 18th PG fuselage stripe and was retired from service in early 1943 following an accident. It is profiled with a fuselage-mounted drop tank attached. The squadron number 106 was reallocated to P-40F-15 serial 41-19836 (see Profile 80).

Profile 78 – P-40F-1 serial 41-14111, squadron number 111

This early P-40F model was First Lieutenant Jack Bade's first Warhawk. It was also among the second batch of fighters assigned at Bauerfield and was assigned to Bade when he arrived with the 44th FS in January 1943. On 13 February 1943 while escorting USN SBD dive-bombers Bade was attacked when flying this aircraft by numerous Zeros rendering his guns unserviceable. Despite a head wound, Bade dove into the Zero formation with jammed guns and was credited with scattering the attackers thus allowing the SBDs to escape. The action earned him the Distinguished Service Cross and Purple Heart. The airframe was written off in early 1943 following an accident and was replaced by the P-40F-15 depicted in Profile 79. The fighter is profiled with a shark mouth and replacement rudder following the 13 February 1943 action.

Profile 79 – P-40F-15 serial 41-198XX (unknown), squadron number 111, *Destitute / Reckless Prostitute*

This long-fuselage P-40F was also assigned to First Lieutenant Jack Bade and crew chief Staff Sergeant James Cooley and following the loss of P-40F-1 41-14111 (see Profile 78, above). The replacement was named *Destitute Prostitute* on the port cowl and *Reckless Prostitute* on the starboard. Bade applied red piping to the white fuselage markings to indicate his status as a flight leader. He eventually flew 85 missions and was credited with five aerial victories. Crew chief Cooley painted fourteen Japanese flags underneath the fighter's starboard side, indicating the cumulative score from all the Warhawks he had maintained.

Profile 80 – P-40F-15 serial 41-19836, squadron number 106, *Peewee*

This long-fuselage P-40F was one of nine P-40F-15s which served with the 44th FS.

PACIFIC PROFILES

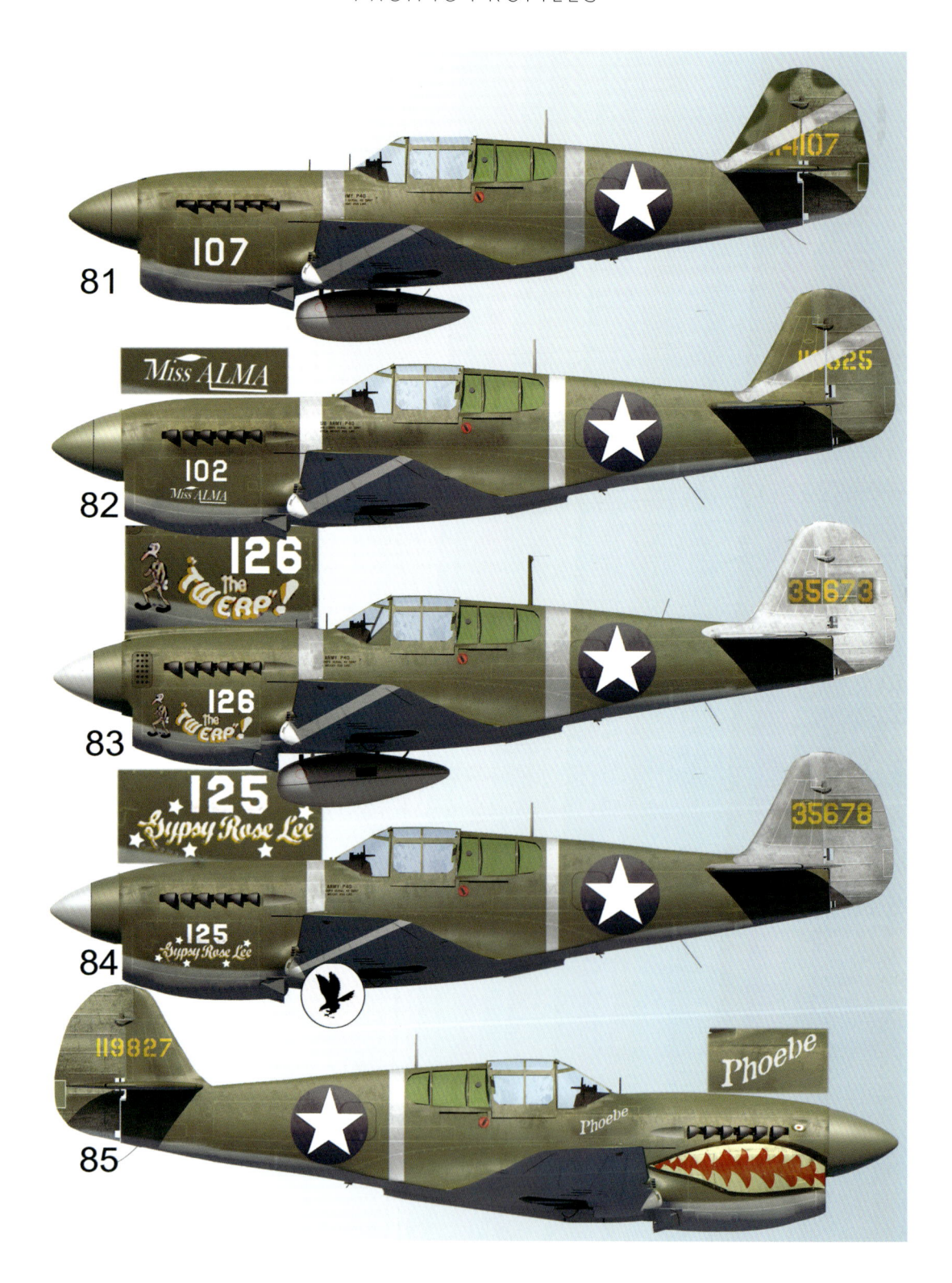

81

82

83

84

85

Profile 81 – P-40F-1 serial 41-14107, squadron number 107

On 14 September 1943 First Lieutenant Andrew Borders went missing after a formation of Warhawks was attacked by Zeros over Bougainville. The formation was returning at 23,000 feet from escorting B-24s making a strike against Kieta. After the war it was confirmed that Borders had baled out and was captured. He was taken to Rabaul where he was later executed on 3 March 1944.

Profile 82 – P-40F-15 serial 41-19825, squadron number 102, *Miss Alma*

This long-fuselage Warhawk was assigned to Captain Hitchcock at Guadalcanal. It replaced the original squadron number 102 being P-40F-1 41-14102 which was reassigned to the 68th FS following an accident.

Profile 83 – P-40M serial 43-5673, squadron number 126, *The Twerp*

This P-40M was assigned to First Lieutenant Frank Gaunt in the second half of 1943. He named it *The Twerp*.

Profile 84 – P-40M serial 43-5678, squadron number 125, *Gypsy Rose Lee*

The P-40M was named *Gypsy Rose Lee* after a famous stripper of the era, due to its stripped-down airframe to improve performance. First Lieutenant Joseph Lesicka claimed five victories in a single mission on 15 July 1943 when flying this fighter. He is acknowledged as the highest scoring 44th FS pilot with nine confirmed victories. He returned to the unit as squadron commander in 1944 by which time it had become a Lightning unit, and later transferred to 18th FG headquarters. Note the diving eagle motif applied to the white wheel hubs.

Profile 85 – P-40F-15 serial 41-19827, (no squadron number), *Phoebe*

This long-fuselage P-40F was transferred to the 44th FS from the 68th FS and retained its shark-mouth markings. It is illustrated before its squadron number was applied. It was flown sometimes by First Lieutenant Lucien "Bob" Shuler who transferred to the squadron from the 68th FS following a bout of malaria. Shuler left the theatre with seven credited victories, four of which were granted on 8 August 1943.

PACIFIC PROFILES

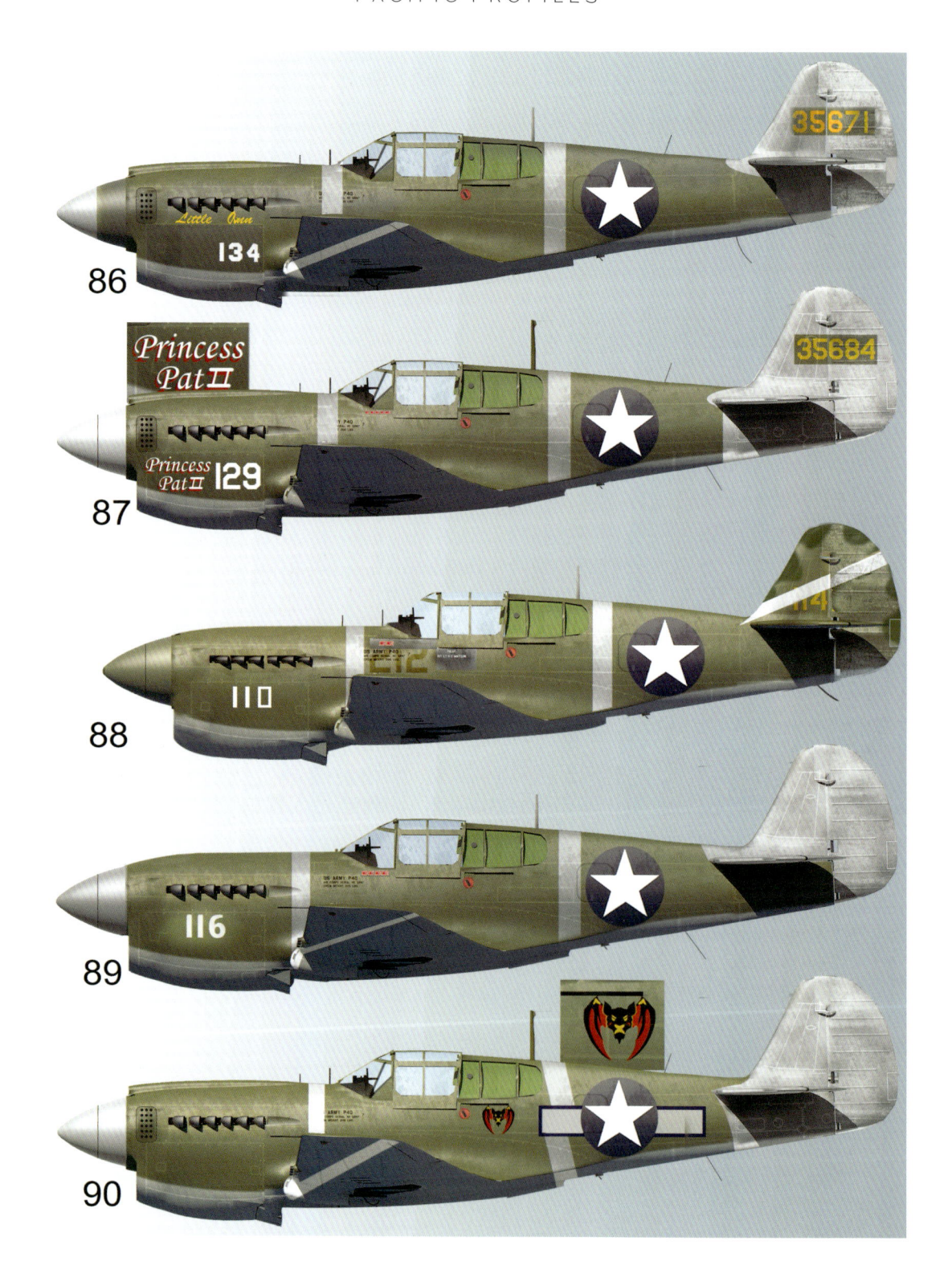

86

87

88

89

90

PAGE 84

Profile 86 – P-40M serial 43-5671, squadron number 134, *Little Anne*

Assigned to First Lieutenant Franklin "Galley" Crain in late 1943, Crain claimed his only kill of the war when flying *Little Anne* on 8 November 1943. That morning the flight controller aboard the destroyer USS *Conway* tasked a combined formation, which included six 44th FS Warhawks led by Captain John Voss, to come to the defence of the ships and beachhead at Torokina. VMF-212 Corsairs first intercepted a formation of incoming Vals and Zeros. During the ensuing fierce and widespread dogfights, Voss was shot down becoming the last Thirteenth Air Force Warhawk pilot lost in action.

Profile 87 – P-40M serial 43-5684, squadron number 129, *Princess Pat II*

Princess Pat II replaced the first *Princess Pat* which was squadron number 104, serial 41-14104. Both were named by Captain Robert Westbrook who named them after a similarly titled popular campfire song of the times. After Westbrook returned to the US, Captain John Voss took over the fighter, however Voss was killed on 8 November over Bougainville in another P-40M as related above. *Princess Pat II* had a cumulative twelve kill flags by the time it was returned to the US for use in warbond drives. It was subsequently destroyed in Arizona on 6 June 1944 during a training accident and is illustrated as it appeared at Munda in late August 1943.

Profile 88 – P-40F-1 serial unknown, squadron number 110

This short-fuselage Warhawk was assigned to First Lieutenant Henry "Mat" Matson who stenciled "1st Lt H.F. Matson" under the cockpit and started a scoreboard forward of the windshield. This aircraft was reassigned into the 44th FS from the 68th FS, and still retained the visible squadron number 212 (painted over) from that unit. The aircraft is illustrated with two Japanese flags, denoting Matson's claims of 28 January and 4 February 1943. This fighter was retired as war-weary around mid-1943 and was replaced by the P-40F-15 illustrated in Profile 89.

Profile 89 – P-40F-15 serial unknown, squadron number 116

This long-fuselage Warhawk replaced First Lieutenant Henry Matson's "110" as illustrated in Profile 88. Matson finished his tour with four official kills. Matson survived a collision in this fighter on 7 June 1943 over the Russell Islands when he collided during combat killing Zero pilot FPO1c Endo Masuaki of No. 251 *Kokutai*.

Profile 90 – P-40M serial unknown, squadron number unknown

Assigned to the care of crew chief Staff Sergeant Ernest Thibodeau, this M model was one of the last to see service in the 44th FS and, exceptionally, carried the new squadron logo on the fuselage. The markings are unique for other reasons too: the white rear band is split and offset, and it is one of very few which had bars added to the US insignia, applied in late 1943. The aircraft is profiled as it appeared at Henderson Field around February 1944, just prior to the conversion to P-38s.

PACIFIC PROFILES

P-40F-15 41-19821 Joan (see Profile 93) in company with P-40F-15 41-19825 Miss Alma from the 44th FS (see Profile 82). They are flying over the lagoon area just to the east of Munda, New Georgia.

Commander of the 68th FS, Major Raymond Williams (circled top left) and his pilots pose at Fighter Two, Guadalcanal, at the end of January 1943. The backdrop P-40F showcases one of the squadron's first sharkmouths. The other circled pilot is First Lieutenant Frederick Ploetz (see Profile 95).

CHAPTER 8
68th Fighter Squadron

The second Thirteenth Air Force squadron to use the Warhawk was the 68th FS. Unlike the 44th FS, it was initially allocated recycled P-40E and E-1s from Australia. The first shipment of 21 P-40E-1s was loaded in crates and shipped from Brisbane. These arrived in Tonga on the Dutch cargo ship *Maetsuycker* on 17 May 1942. The squadron was one of those assigned to protect the Pacific ferry route from Japanese carrier attack and was based at Tongatabu airfield in the Kingdom of Tonga. It was assigned to the 347th FG. The 68th FS lost two Warhawks and pilots to accidents during its Tonga deployment. The unit remained there until 28 October 1942, before its ground echelon moved to Tontouta, New Caledonia, without aircraft on 2 November 1942.

At Tontouta its pilots were attached to the 67th FS where they trained in Airacobras. However, the 68th FS was re-equipped with P-40Fs which they ferried to Guadalcanal on Christmas Day 1942, setting up base at Fighter Two. Back at Tonga the squadron's original seventeen remaining P-40E-1s and one orphan P-40K were transferred to No.15 Squadron, RNZAF, on 27 October 1942. The P-40E-1s were assigned RNZAF serials NZ3091 to NZ3107 with the orphan P-40K-1 rebadged as NZ3108.

The 68th FS operated Warhawks and then Airacobras throughout the Solomons campaign. The squadron swapped over their Warhawk inventory for P-39s in June 1943 at Tontouta, transferring their more serviceable Warhawks to the 44th FS. Several of its pilots were seconded to P-38 units in early 1943 to gain Lockheed Lightning experience, however the unit did not convert to the type until August 1944 after the squadron had left the theatre. As such the unit operated only P-40Fs in combat, both short and long-fuselage versions.

Markings

The 68th FS's first batch of short-fuselage P-40F-1s commenced the squadron numbering sequence at 201, continuing in the two-hundred series, with the highest known allocated squadron number being 257. The first batch of long-fuselage P-40F-15s spread throughout the serial range 41-19819 to 41-19844 was delivered to the 68th FS at Guadalcanal in January 1943. Similar to the 44th FS, white identification vertical bands were added to the forward and rear fuselage, and the forward fuselage ones extended on the top and under surface of the wing. These were replaced in late June 1943 with an all-white tail, thus these markings replicated those of its sister 44th FS. Although the shark-mouth marking was unique to the 68th FS, regular airframe swaps ensured shark-mouths appeared in both inventories, particularly after the squadron's entire serviceable Warhawk inventory was transferred to the 44th FS in mid-June 1943. Each shark mouth was individual in shape, varied in size considerably, and started appearing on airframes as early as January 1943.

Note that the 68th FS emblem, featuring a knight riding lightning bolts, was not approved until 29 November 1944, and hence was not extant during the Warhawk era. It was created later to reflect the squadron as a P-38 unit.

PACIFIC PROFILES

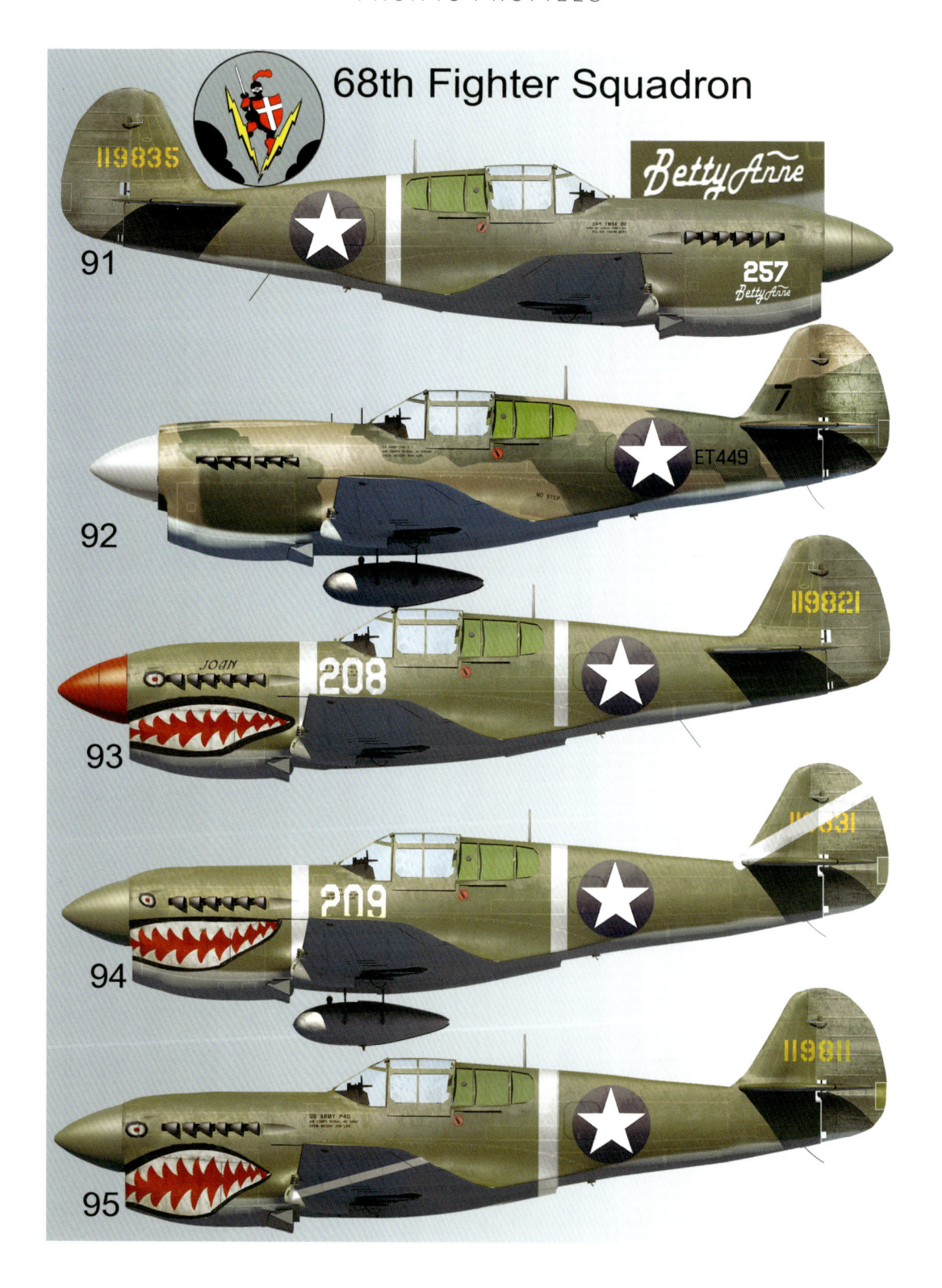

68th Fighter Squadron

91 — 119835 "Betty Anne" 257

92 — ET449 7

93 — 119821 208 "JOAN"

94 — 119831 209

95 — 119811

Profile 91 – P-40F-15 serial 41-19835, squadron number 257, *Betty Anne*

This fighter is profiled as it appeared at Guadalcanal's Fighter Two around February 1943 before the white tail, wing and forward fuselage stripe theatre markings were applied.

Profile 92 – P-40E-1 serial 41-25125, British Serial ET449, squadron number 7

This fighter served with the 68th FS in Tonga after which it was transferred to No. 15 Squadron, RNZAF, on 27 October 1942 at Fua'amotu. The two hundred series squadron numbers did not begin until the unit departed Tonga in late 1942 and was issued with P-40Fs.

Profile 93 – P-40F-15 serial 41-19821, squadron number 208, *Joan*

This fighter is profiled as it appeared in the Solomons theatre around April 1943. Squadron numbers were stencilled in large white stencils underneath the cockpit.

Profile 94 – P-40F-15 serial 41-19831, squadron number 209

This fighter is profiled as it appeared in the Solomons theatre as assigned to Second Lieutenant Lucien "Bob" Shuler in April 1943. He flew 33 combat missions with the 68th FS between February and May 1943, after which malaria grounded him. After three weeks of treatment, Shuler subsequently transferred to the 44th FS where he was assigned a P-40M named *Georgia Peach*.

Profile 95 – P-40F-15 serial 41-19811

This Warhawk was assigned to First Lieutenant Frederick Ploetz and is profiled before it was allocated a squadron number at Fighter Two in February 1943. Ploetz flew this fighter for his only aerial victory awarded on 20 January 1943.

Second Lieutenant "Bob" Shuler flies P-40F-15 41-19831, as illustrated in Profile 94, over Guadalcanal. Note the underwing white theatre markings include the tailplane under surface.

P-40F-15 41-19835 Betty Anne, the subject of Profile 91, parked against the southern hill-line at Guadalcanal's' Fighter Two.

P-40F-15 41-19831, as illustrated in Profile 94, flies along Guadalcanal's northern coastline, with Tulagi in the background.

The shark-mouth of P-40F-15 41-19821, as shown in Profile 93, at Guadalcanal just before squadron number 208 was applied.

The Green Banana was an earlier N model transferred into the 110th TRS.

P-40N-20 43-23198, as illustrated in Profile 97, over New Guinea's northern coast.

CHAPTER 9
110th Tactical Reconnaissance Squadron "Musketeers"

The 110th TRS arrived at Brisbane on 5 December 1943 aboard the transport ship *Cape Mendocino* led by Major William Lowgan. Its pilots were later assigned to the 35th Fighter Group at Port Moresby's Durand and Schwimmer 'dromes to conduct familiarisation and in-country training. It entered combat in the New Guinea theatre with about two dozen P-39N and Q model Airacobras. The 110th TRS redeployed to Tadji from Gusap in June 1944 where it helped mop up Japanese forces around the Wewak area. On 11 September 1944 the unit moved to Biak, however just prior to the move the first P-40Ns were assigned into the squadron at Tadji to commence replacement of the aging Airacobra inventory.

Markings

In March 1944 the Fifth Air Force declared the P-40N and all pre-models as fit only for training purposes due to ample availability of more modern types such as the P-38, P-47 and P-51. The last N models delivered in August 1944 were assigned to Fifth Fighter Command, with the balance of the extant 49th FG P-40N inventory was reassigned to the 110th TRS. Whilst these P-40Ns would later fly in the Philippines, they nonetheless appeared briefly in the New Guinea theatre at the end of 1944. The unit used squadron numbers 10-35.

The 110th TRS logo featured the head of a caricatured black and white mule, with red eyes and brown goggles, against a backdrop of two crossed machine-guns. When the unit later converted to P-51s in the Philippines it changed its name and logo to the *Flying Musketeers*.

P-40N-20 squadron number 10, as seen in Profile 96, at Tadji.

110th Tactical Reconnaissance Squadron

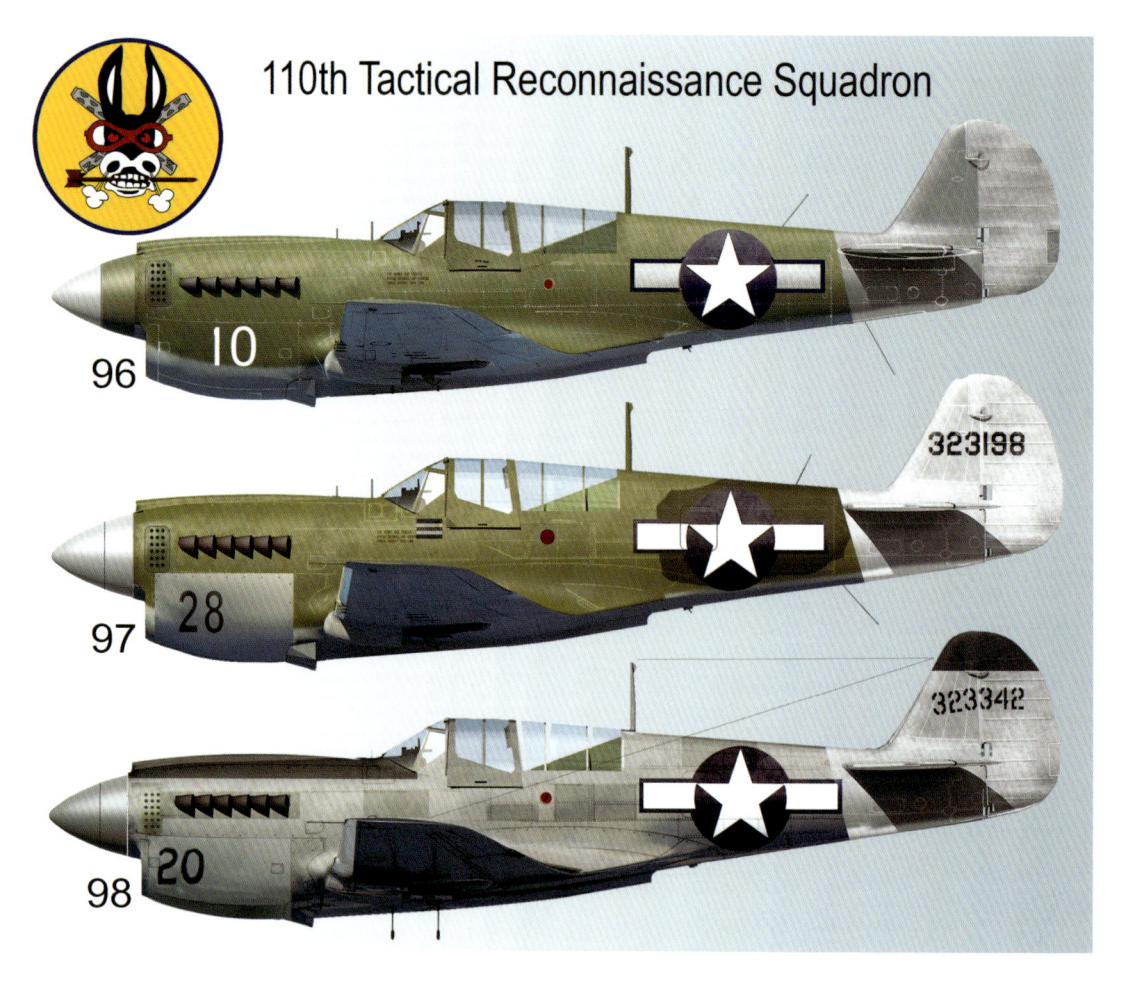

Profile 96 – P-40N-20 serial unknown, squadron number 10
This fighter transferred into the 110th TRS from the 49th FG in 1944.

Profile 97 – P-40N-20 serial 43-23198, squadron number 28
This fighter transferred into the 110th TRS from the 49th FG with a replacement cowl.

Profile 98 – P-40N-20 serial 43-23342, squadron number 20
This P-40N-20 was transferred from the RAAF in August 1944 where it previously served as A29-678. It had been delivered to Australia in December 1943 but did not see squadron service before being transferred to the USAAF as part of a reverse Lend Lease transaction.

P-40N-20 43-23342, the subject of Profile 98, at Morotai, just after leaving the New Guinea theatre.

Captain Richard "Pinky" Wilson sits in P-40N-5 Anne III, as seen in Profile 101, at Gusap.

The unusual P-40E with the mistaken "1501" serial, as detailed in Profile 104, inside a Port Moresby hangar after conversion to a two-seater in mid to late 1944.

The modified two-seater P-40E 41-5481 (as illustrated in Profile 104) in the Hollandia "boneyard" in late 1944, with the tail now painted white.

CHAPTER 10
312th Bombardment Group

The four squadrons in this bombardment group only briefly used the Warhawk in New Guinea as an interim measure until they took delivery of Douglas A-20Gs. The group trained as a dive-bomber unit on Vultee Vengeances in the US. Due to a shortage of A-20G light bombers at the time, the group was initially assigned to Fifth Fighter Command when it arrived in Australia in late 1943 where its squadrons were issued with new P-40N-5s shortly after their arrival. The group's pilots commenced flying practice from Archerfield in Brisbane where the first nose-art was applied by an RAAF sergeant. After ferrying their P-40Ns to New Guinea, the 312th BG saw three weeks of flying operations with the P-40Ns at Gusap. Following this the Warhawks were transferred to the 49th FG, also stationed there. The 312th BG pilots then returned to Port Moresby for transition training to A-20Gs.

Major William "Bill" Kemble's P-40N-5 42-105854, as depicted in Profile 103, after it was shot up by Ki-43-IIs north of Gusap.

PACIFIC PROFILES

386th, 387th, 388th & 389th Bombardment Squadrons

99

100

101

102

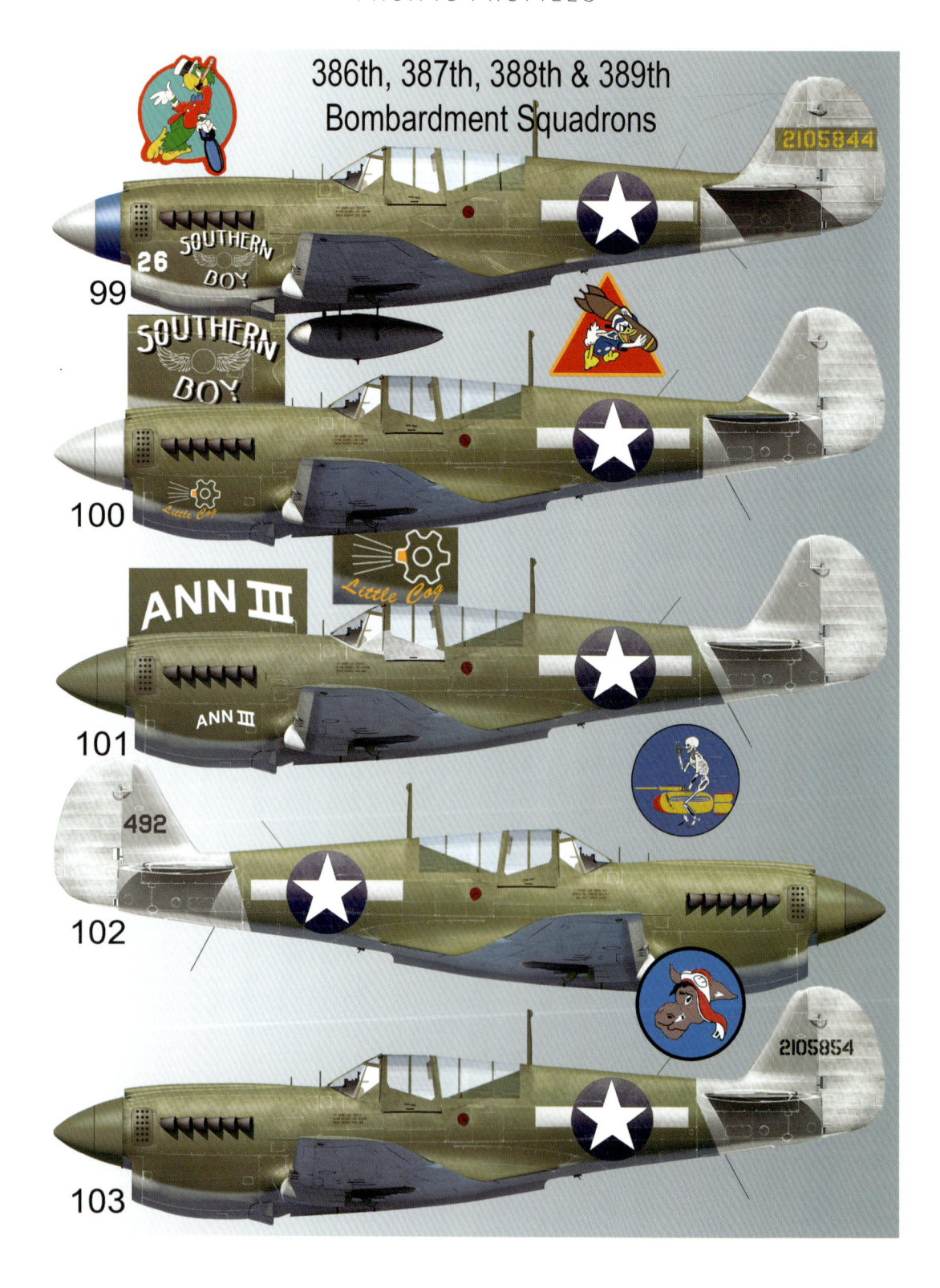

103

Profile 99 – P-40N-5 serial 42-105844, squadron number 26, *Southern Boy*, 387th BS

From Florida, First Lieutenant Bill Pagh named his Warhawk *Southern Boy*. The fighter was later transferred to the 7th FS where it was named *Alabam West Anniston Rambler*. After transitioning to A-20Gs at Port Moresby, Pagh was promoted to captain, and made commander of the 387th BS. He was lost over Utarom, New Guinea on 11 August 1944 flying a brand-new A-20G which he had only the day prior named *Florida Gator*. The 387th BS Joe Carioca squadron logo appears above the profile.

Profile 100 – P-40N-5 serial unknown, *Little Cog*, 386th BS

First Lieutenant Larry Folmar named his assigned fighter *Little Cog* due to his perceived role in the war. Folmar ferried this fighter from Archerfield near Brisbane to Gusap over three days, departing on 10 December 1943. The 386th BS Donald Duck squadron logo appears above the profile.

Profile 101 – P-40N-5 serial unknown, *Anne III*, 386th BS

This fighter was operated by the 386th BS commander Captain Richard "Pinky" Wilson at Gusap.

Profile 102 – P-40N-5 serial 42-105492, 389th BS

This fighter was assigned to the 389th BS commander Major Selmon Wells at Gusap. The last three digits of the serial number were stencilled over the white tail theatre marking. The 389th BS skeleton riding a bomb appears above the profile.

Profile 103 – P-40N-5 serial 42-105854, 388th BS

On 15 January 1944, this Warhawk was shot up by 59th *Sentai* Ki-43-II Oscar fighters when flown by the 388th BS Commander, Major William "Bill" Kemble. It force-landed at Gusap where it suffered an undercarriage failure and was written off for spares. The 388th BS logo featuring a goggled mule appears above the profile.

First Lieutenant Bill Pagh with P-40N-5 Southern Boy, the subject of Profile 99, at Gusap.

P-40N-20 serial 43-23187, as shown in Profile 108, following a landing mishap at Townsville in mid-1944.

Former 8th FS P-40E-1, the subject of Profile 106, cruises over cloudy New Guinea skies near Port Moresby in early 1944.

CHAPTER 11
Unique Warhawks

Profiles 104 to 110 illustrate Warhawks which have either a unique history or markings as indicated.

Two P-40s parked at Nadzab with a P-47 behind. The Warhawk on the left is P-40E serial 41-5329, as illustrated in Profile 105.

Profile 104 – P-40E serial 41-5481, (customer 41/501), various units 1942/44

In its later life this Warhawk appeared at Port Moresby with "1501" stencilled under the tailplane. A logical conclusion leads to P-40E serial 41-501, however the number derives from shipment 41/501. This designation means it was the 501st P-40E built for a certain 1941 Curtiss-Wright customer that year, in this case the customer being the Soviet Union. This Warhawk left the factory without a serial as part of the protocol which required it to be stripped of any US identification as governed by pre-war neutrality laws.

PACIFIC PROFILES

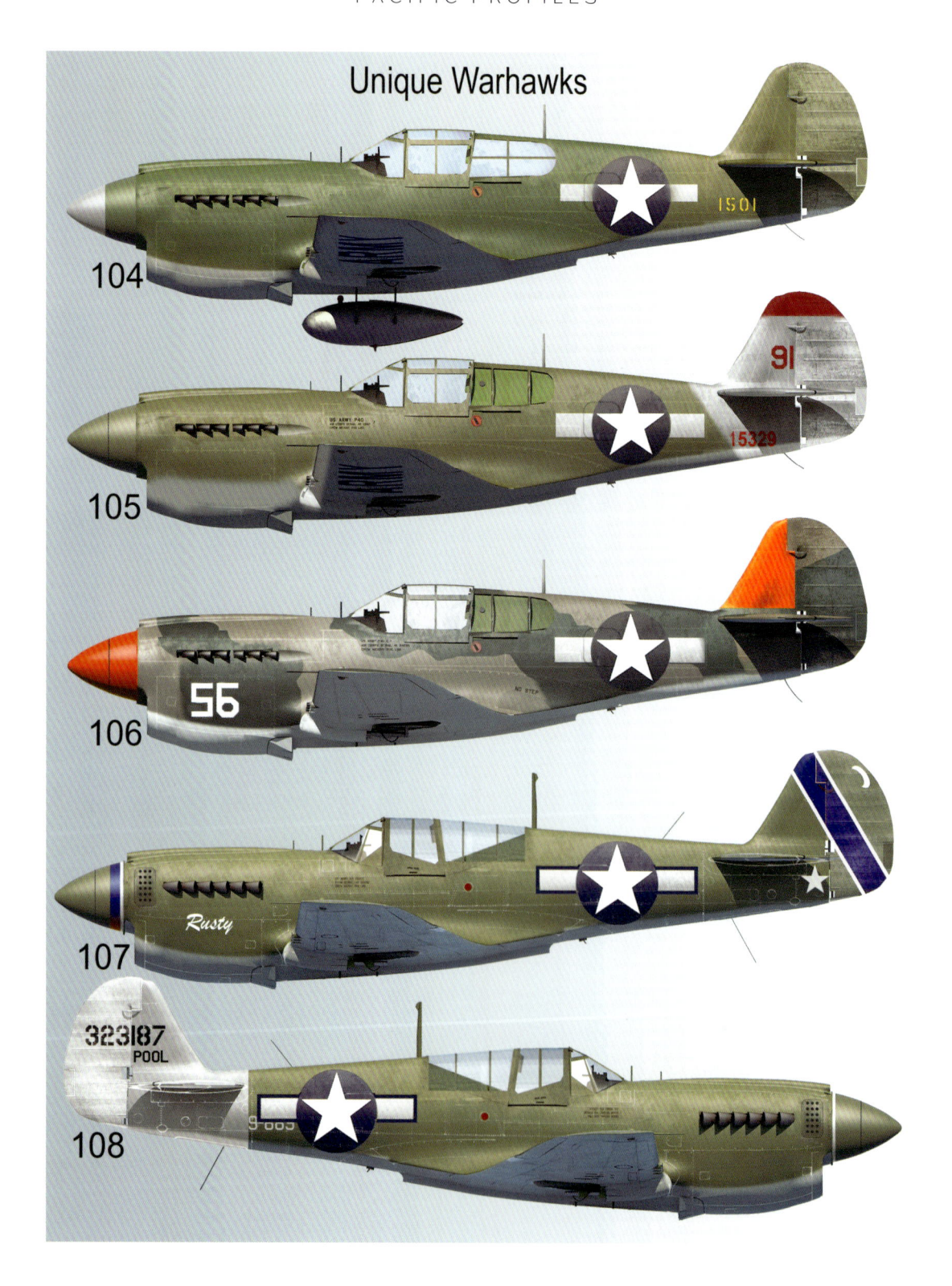

Unique Warhawks

104

105

106

107

108

PAGE 102

The aircraft was instead rebadged as P-40E serial 41-5481 and diverted to Australia. It was assigned to the 8th FS in Darwin where it was flown by Lieutenant Charles Johnson (see Profile 38). He belly landed the fighter on 4 June 1942, and its transfer documentation identified it as "501" which was misinterpreted as serial 41-501. Between mid to late 1943 "1501" was converted into two-seat configuration by the 27th Air Deport at Port Moresby to become a photo platform for Fifth Fighter Command. It remained in this role until it was struck off charge in October 1944. The aircraft is illustrated shortly after its conversion, where foliage green was applied to the forward airframe.

Profile 105 – P-40E serial 41-5329, squadron number 91, 342nd FS

Assigned into the 7th FS on 6 March 1942, this early P-40E eventually found its way into the 342nd FS, a P-47D Thunderbolt unit which utilised it as a hack at Nadzab. It is profiled as it appeared there in March 1944 where it became one of the few E models with a white leading edge and white tailplane theatre markings. The serial was stencilled underneath the tailplane in red.

Profile 106 – P-40E-1 serial unknown, squadron number 56

This P-40E-1 at first served with the 8th FS at Darwin before moving to Dobodura, but by early 1944 it had been placed with the 27th Air Depot at Port Moresby. The previous squadron number 56 was retained on the cowl, and the spinner and top half of the fin was painted bright orange to identify the aircraft.

Profile 107 – P-40N-20 serial unknown, *Rusty*, 418th Night Fighter Squadron

An advanced detachment of the 418th NFS arrived in New Guinea in November 1943. The unit's first four P-61A Black Widows did not arrive until 21 April 1944, with the squadron told to expect lengthy night intruder missions using the range of the Black Widow. Squadron commander Captain William Sellers acquired this P-40N for combat training purposes which he named *Rusty* after his young son. Sellers' purpose in the training was to underline the difficulty of shaking an attacker without the security of another P-61 as wingman. The new P-61As acquired the crescent and star with oblique blue band with white piping as a squadron insignia on their fins which Sellers also applied to his Warhawk. The blue band and white piping was replicated on the spinner.

Profile 108 – P-40N-20 serial 43-23187, Far East Air Force Training Pool

This P-40N was delivered to Australia in February 1944 and was allocated RAAF serial A29-689. In August 1944 it was transferred to the FEAF as part of a reverse Lend-Lease transaction. It was used by the FEAF Training Pool at Townsville, replacing the combat-worn inventory of P-40E/E-1s and Ks serving there at the time. The fighter is profiled as it appeared at Garbutt in September 1944.

Profile 109 – P-40N-5 serial 42-105499, squadron number 26

This Warhawk was a rare case in the 49th FG whereby its serial number was re-stenciled over the theatre white tail marking. Flight Leader First Lieutenant Lawrence "Larry" Succop was lost flying this fighter in New Guinea on 17 October 1943. Succop was leading three 7th FS P-40Ns as they climbed to intercept incoming Zeros, in an attempt to join a formation of 475th FG Lightnings above them. They struggled to do so, however, and were bounced from behind by a massive force of sixty Zeros from Nos. 204 and 253 *Kokutai*. While his wingmen dived away, Succop was last seen over Cape Ward Hunt. In addition to Succop, the Zeros shot down four Lightnings in exchange for eight Zeros lost.

Profile 110 – P-40M serial 43-5699, squadron number 99

This airframe was reassigned to the Fifth Air Force Fighter Command from the 44th FS in the Solomons after that unit converted to the Lockheed Lightning. It was the only M Model to serve with the 49th FG and was assigned to group commander Lieutenant Colonel David Campbell. He was flying this fighter when he claimed his fourth and final kill of the war, on 13 March 1944 over Wewak. Note that the fuselage white band Solomons theatre markings have been painted over although the wing undersurfaces ones were retained.

SOURCES & ACKNOWLEDGMENTS

Research for this volume draws on primary sources. The author's extensive collection of photos and notes from field trips contributes considerable but interlinking minutiae accumulated over the years. A special thanks go, in particular, to two Australian aviation historians, Gordon Birkett and Craig "Buzz" Busby. Both are experts in the Australian P-40 era and both willingly shared their expertise. Gordon also took time to proof much of the text. Other sources are cited below.

ADF serials website adf-serials.com.au

Aircraft Movements, Townsville Control Tower, 1942-45

Allied Air Force Intelligence Summaries 1942/4 (Australian War Memorial)

Allied Translator and Interpreter Section (ATIS) Reports

ANGAU patrol officer reports of Allied crash sites 1940s-1970s

Curtiss-Wright - P-40 technical construction drawings and markings guides

Curtiss-Wright Aircraft Corporation - historic records - numerous

Curtiss-Wright Factory Representative Reports, 1943/44

Field Trips by author throughout Pacific, 1964-2017

Fighter Command Replacement Centre (FCRC) – establishment

Headquarters COMAIRSOL Special Markings Orders

Headquarters Fifth Air Force Special Markings & Revocation Orders

P-40 markings details from relevant Individual Deceased Personnel Files (IDPF)

Pacific Aircraft Historical Society - Wreck Data Sheets

Pacificwrecks Website www.pacificwrecks.com and its diligent administrator, Justin Taylan

Papua New Guinea Catholic Mission Association, Field Trips of, Papua New Guinea

PNG Colonial Office - Civil Administration Records

PNG Museum of Modern History

RAAF/ USAAF replacement pool Charters Towers – inventory records

Microfilms: Official Unit Records & Maintenance Sheets

Fifth and Thirteenth AF Units via Maxwell AFB: 5th Air Force Establishment, Fifth Fighter Command, Thirteenth Fighter Command, 13th Air Force Establishment, 312th BG, 8th FG, 49th FG, 18th FG, 347th FG, 35th FS, 4th Air Depot, 27th Air Depot, 8th FS, 9th FS, 35th FS, 68th FS, 44th FS, 110th FS, 386th BS, 419th NFS, 387th BS, 388th BS & 389th BS.

INDEX OF NAMES

Index of Names
Allen, 1st Lt David 37
Alsop, Lt Thomas 71
Angel, 2nd Lt James 65, 66
Archerbald, 2nd Lt James 30
Aubrey, 1st Lt Carl 37
Bade, 1st Lt Jack 81
Ball, 2nd Lt Edward 30
Barnett, 1st Lt Clyde 47, 49
Blanton, Capt Nathaniel 29, 39
Boermann, Lt Fred 73
Borders, 1st Lt Andrew 83
Brewer, Lt James 73
Brownell, 2nd Lt Nelson 1
Buel, Lt Robert 27
Campbell, Lt Col David 104
Cooley, S/Sgt James 78, 81
Crain, 1st Lt Franklin 85
Davis, Major Emmett 69, 73
Day, Lt William 49, 54
Dennis, 1st Lt Richard 49
Dillworth, 2nd Lt Harry 37
Disney, Walt 76
Docksteder, Lt RC 45
Donalson, Lt Jack 59, 63
Eisenberg, Lt Monroe 47
Endo Masuaki, FPO1c 85
Farrell, Capt Roger 39
Fielder, Lt Arthur 47
Fisher, 2nd Lt John 3
Finberg, 2nd Lt Floyd 63
Flack, Lt Nelson 47
Folmar, 1st Lt Larry 99
Francis, 2nd Lt Russell 65
Gaunt, 1st Lt Frank 74, 79, 83
Geiss, Lieutenant Carl 24
George, General Hal 33
Glover, 2nd Lt John 22, 27
Goltry, M/Sgt Lynman 27
Hanning, 1st Lt William 30
Hansen, 2nd Lt Larry 35
Harris, Capt Ernest 51, 53
Harvey, 2nd Lt Clyde 61, 63
Head, Lt Cotesworth 74
Hennon, Capt Bill 29, 33
Hillard, Lt Ray 39
Hitchcock, Capt 83

Hollier, 2nd Lt Frederick 59
Holly, 2nd Lt Austin 30
House, 2nd Lt Arthur T Jr 31, 33
Howard, Robert 49
Hutchinson, Lt Col Donald 29, 30
Irvin, Capt Ben 57, 65, 66
Jackson, 2nd Lt Warren 30
Jacoby, Melvin 33
Jarmen, 2nd Lt Logan 7
Johnson, Lt Charles 51, 103
Johnson, Lt Lester 29, 37
Keator, Capt Randall 51
Kemble, Major William 97, 99
King, 2nd Lt Joseph 35
Kiser, 1st Lt George 27, 45, 47, 55
Klandrud, 1st Lt Roy 71
Knisley, 1st Lt Clyde 35
Kruzel, 2nd Lt Joseph 27, 57, 59
Landers, 1st Lt John 59, 63, 65
Lee, 1st Lt Donald 37
Lesicka, 1st Lt Joseph 83
Levitan, 1st Lt Bill 61
Little, Major John 75
Littleton, Lt Joe 53
Lowgan, Major William 93
Lynd, Lt Cyrus 65
MacArthur, General 23
Martin, 2nd Lt Harold 35
Martin, 2nd Lt Harvey 47
Matson, 1st Lt Henry 85
McClelland, Major Harold 69
McComsey, 1st Lt Robert 56, 59
McMahon, Lt Robert 24, 25, 27
Melikan, Capt Ray 37
Meuten, 1st Lt Donald 53
Moore, Capt Dan 53
Morehead, Lt Jim 45
Morrissey, Lt Col Robert 29, 30, 33, 35
Musial, Lt John 47
Nichols, Capt Frank 35, 37
Nolan, Sgt Jerry 73
O'Riley, 2nd Lt Frederick 29
Oestreicher, Lt Robert 24, 27
Pagh, 1st Lt Bill 99
Paris, Lt Joel 39
Parker, Lt Robert 71
Peaselee, Jesse 57

Pell, Major Floyd 24
Petersen, 1st Lt Clayton 59
Pierce, Lt Samuel 49, 53
Pixey, Capt Victor 57
Ploetz, 1st Lt Frederick 86, 89
Poleschuk, 2nd Lt Stephan 63
Pollock, Lt Gene 39
Preddy, 1st Lt George 61
Prentice, Major George 33
Props, 2nd Lt Chris 37
Reynolds, Lt Andrew 57, 59, 65
Selman, Col James 29, 57, 61
Sellers, Capt William 103
Shelton, Sgt Ray 71
Shuler, 1st Lt Lucien 83, 89
Sims, Capt Mitchell 45, 49
Souther, 1st Lt Harold 69, 71, 108
Sprague, Major Charles 24, 27
Stanton, 1st Lt Arland 35
Stonacker, 1st Lt "Red" 71
Strauss, Capt Allison 45
Succop, 1st Lt Lawrence 104
Suers, Lt Richard 24
Takala, Lt Neil 47
Taylor, 2nd Lt Deems 61
Thibodeau, S/Sgt Ernest 85
Thorvaldson, 1st Lt Joel 53
Tice, 1st Lt Clay 59
Tyler, Major Kermit 75
Tyler, Lt JW 33
Van Auken, Capt Robert 29, 45
Vargas, Alberto 37
Vaught, Lt Robert 59, 65, 67
Vodra, 1st Lt Richard 51
Vodrey, Lt Oliver 29, 33
Voss, Capt John 85
Watkins, 1st Lt James 61
Wells, Major Selmon 99
Wesley, 2nd Lt Bryant 30, 33
West, Lt Richard 71
Westbrook, Major Robert 75, 85
Williams, Major Raymond 86
Wilmarth, 2nd Lt Clarence 30
Wire, 2nd Lt Ralph 59
Wilson, Capt Richard 95, 99
Woods, Lt Sid 65
Wurtsmith, Major Paul 29, 30, 63

Underlining the ingenuity and determination of Fifth Air Force engineers to recover airframes, this P-40 is in the process of being recovered from a swamp near Dobodura on 21 September 1943 following a take-off accident.

Pilot First Lieutenant Harold Souther fills out an accident report on the wing of P-40N 42-105519 (the subject of profile 68) following a landing mishap at Finschhafen. Although the damage looks superficial, the aircraft was written off and stripped for parts. It was replaced by the 35th Fighter Squadron's only M model, in turn transferred from the Thirteenth Air Force via Australia. Note the airframe carries the numeral 4 instead of its original letter H. This numeral was applied following a previous repair when another Warhawk was allocated H, and the 35th FS started using numerals when it ran out of Roman letters.